Junior NKIERE MAKOLONI

Information and communication techniques course 7th EB

Junior NKIERE MAKOLONI

Information and communication techniques course 7th EB

ScienciaScripts

Imprint
Any brand names and product names mentioned in this book are subject to trademark, brand or patent protection and are trademarks or registered trademarks of their respective holders. The use of brand names, product names, common names, trade names, product descriptions etc. even without a particular marking in this work is in no way to be construed to mean that such names may be regarded as unrestricted in respect of trademark and brand protection legislation and could thus be used by anyone.

Cover image: www.ingimage.com

This book is a translation from the original published under ISBN 978-620-6-72582-4.

Publisher:
Sciencia Scripts
is a trademark of
Dodo Books Indian Ocean Ltd. and OmniScriptum S.R.L publishing group

120 High Road, East Finchley, London, N2 9ED, United Kingdom
Str. Armeneasca 28/1, office 1, Chisinau MD-2012, Republic of Moldova, Europe
Managing Directors: Ieva Konstantinova, Victoria Ursu
info@omniscriptum.com

Printed at: see last page
ISBN: 978-620-8-51176-0

Contents

PREFACE

For some years now, the world has been undergoing change as a result of a high-speed evolution in the use and perfection of new information and communication technologies, which are now visible in almost every area of life. IT is currently used in companies as part of an information and production system.

As defined in the Larousse dictionary, computing is the science of rational and automatic information processing; computing is considered to be a medium of knowledge in various fields of science. Computers are currently used for control, surveillance, communication and many other applications that we will never be able to list in their entirety, just to show how broad their field application is.

IT is not a miracle cure for all the company's ills; however, when used rationally within the framework of a pre-established organisation with the partners concerned, it can appear as a tool for development. development tool.

In order to do this, we must first provide training for our students who wish to pursue their professional careers in public administration, by writing appropriate books that will enable them to study well and acquire a basic knowledge of computing. This is the aim of this book on computing for students in the third year of the Humanities, secretarial-administration option.

Although NICTs are much more widely used in companies, schools and other educational institutions are showing a need for the use of this tool, particularly technical schools.

We would like to thank the Haut-Uélé Provincial Ministry of Education and the Haut-Uélé 2 Provincial Inspectorate for their involvement in the implementation of this project, which will benefit not only the Haut-Uélé Province but all the schools in our country.

SUMMARY

This theoretical and practical book, which is easy to understand for pupils in the seventh year of basic education, will also serve as a compendium for teachers who want to learn about computers, as it conforms to the national curriculum for primary, secondary and technical education in the Democratic Republic of Congo. In this book we have focused on concepts such : mastery of general concepts of computing, presentation of the computer, discovering computer peripherals, the fundamentals of Windows, directory files, search engine browsers, the various Internet sites, use of e-mail, attachments and handling MS Word.
If you follow the teaching in this book through to the end, you'll be well on your way to the sixth year of the humanities, and you'll no longer have any problems following up the concepts covered in the fourth year of the humanities.
We look forward to receiving your comments, criticisms and any suggestions you may have for improving this book, and we encourage every school to buy a copy. By purchasing a copy, you are encouraging scientific research.
Our gratitude goes entirely to Jesus Christ, who has given us victory over sin.

OBJECTIVE

GENERAL OBJECTIVE

The general aim of this course is to provide Year 7 EB students with a theoretical and practical grounding in the basics of computing.

SPECIFIC OBJECTIVES

At the end of this course, any student who follows it assiduously will be able to :

- Master the general concepts of computing;
- Introducing the computer ;
- Discovering computer peripherals ;
- Demonstrate the fundamentals of Windows ;
- Distinguish between ;
- Differentiating between search engine browsers ;
- Mastering different websites;
- Using e-mail ;
- Exploiting attachments ;
- Handling MS Word.

CHAPTER I

GENERAL CONCEPTS OF COMPUTING

I.1 GENERAL INFORMATION ABOUT COMPUTERS

I.1.1.DEFINITION

Computing is the science of automatic and rational information processing.

I.1.2.BACKGROUND

The word 'informatique' (computer science) was coined by Philippe Dreyfus, director of Bull's Centre national de calcul électronique (National Electronic Computing Centre), in 1962. It is in fact a neologism in the French language resulting from the contraction of the two words "automatique" and "information" to refer to the automatic processing of information.

Computing spread over the 19th and 20th centuries and is linked to the appearance of the first automata. Charles Babbage is considered to be the grandfather of modern computers, having invented the analytical machine in 1834. This was a programmable calculating machine. Unfortunately, Babbage never saw the machine in his lifetime, as the British Crown was fed up with the lengthy research and withdrew its financial support.

ENIAC, one of the first computers ever built.

The evolution of programming languages

With regard to generations of computers, it is possible to draw parallels between types of software. For example, the first generation of computers involved direct machine coding in binary; the second, assembly language; the third, advanced languages (Fortran, Cobol, Simula, APL, etc.); the fourth, second-generation advanced languages such as Pascal and C++, known as 'structured', as well as 'object' languages and very high-level query such as SQL. A Japanese fifth-generation project was launched by MITI in the very early 1980s and was to be based around inference engines and the Prolog language, but despite substantial funding, the project never came to fruition.

A LITTLE CHRONOLOGY

- First generation: from relays to lamps
- Second generation: transistors
- Third generation: integrated circuits
- Fourth generation: microcomputers
- Fifth generation: graphic interface and networks

THE FIRST USES

Initially, IT had two main uses: scientific computing (for both civilian and military purposes, stimulated by the Cold War) and business management support, taking over from mechanography. In English, there are two distinct fields: Computer Science and Information Systems.
The end of the 1960s was marked by a speculative bubble in electronics due to the appearance of large-scale integrated circuits and, above all, new ways using computers, particularly time-sharing on remote terminals.
New machines make it possible automate calculations previously carried out by pools of human calculators in companies, universities and research organisations. The US Department of Defense has subsidised major research programmes in programming, pattern recognition and artificial intelligence, coding and cryptography, and automatic language translation, all of which have enabled computer applications to take off.
In France, on a smaller scale, in the mid-1960s, the diversification of applications was combined with the attraction of computers for various scientific projects (from logic to linguistics). But it would be more than ten years before the major scientific institutions officially accepted the idea that computing was a new science.
The artist Vera Molnár has been using computers and algorithmic art in her artistic creations since 1968.

THE INTRODUCTION OF IT INTO SOCIETY

With the increasing power and reliability of computers, all social practices involving research, design, manufacture, marketing, publication and communication have been invaded and transformed by computing. Micro-computing has enabled a wide distribution components microprocessor-based information systems in technical systems and the creation of microcomputers. The networks

This made it possible to decentralise machines close to workstations and to introduce the first cross-machine communications. Manufacturers designed architectures to connect them, such as DSA (CII-Honeywell-Bull), DEC's Decnet and IBM's SNA.

I.1.3.THE IMPORTANCE OF INFORMATION TECHNOLOGY IN SOCIETY

These days, computers are everywhere - a veritable epidemic! Whether in shops, bars, vending machines, petrol stations, schools, libraries, airports or at work, nothing works without it. "IT and the Internet on every floor" you might say, and if not, there's always the cyber café!

Families have had to adapt to this new reality. Now everything is done over the internet, no more paper letters. People no longer give their postal address, but rather their email address.

It's true that IT tools allow us to present our written work in an excellent way, and that the Internet is a fantastic means of communicating with the rest of the world, like SKYPE, Email, Google, Yahoo, but also, being able to scan or print!

Thanks to the Internet, you can, among other things, chat with friends anywhere in the world, find information on any subject, publish a text with multimedia effects, listen to music, watch films, enrol on courses and even follow them virtually, download or share photos, meet people from different cultures, check your bank accounts and make payments, track your telephone use at any time of the day or night, buy and sell almost anything, and so on. It also helps you in a number of other areas of your life:

- Medicine: doctors can obtain information on new medicines and treatments, Health check-up
- Aviation: pilots can communicate with each other remotely via control towers
- Journalism: journalists can publish reports on websites
- Hotels: customers can book their hotel rooms.
- Teaching: teachers and students can carry out documentary research.
- Historians can research the past.
- The Library: the librarian can list, classify and locate books.
- Architecture: the architect can draw up model plans for the construction of buildings.
- The Bank: the banker can transfer money through money exchange services.

However, it's important to control the amount of time you spend surfing the Internet, because too much can lead to social problems (with friends and family), back pain, vision problems and even obesity. On the other hand, we mustn't forget that there are wonderful things in life a computer can't provide: contact, perfume, a social life, etc.

1.2. GENERAL CONCEPTS OF COMPUTING

1.2.1. THE CONCEPT OF AN ALGORITHM

In computing, an algorithm is **the description of a sequence of steps used to obtain a result from input elements**.

The concept of algorithm is the oldest, since 2500 years before our era, accountants were already using algorithms to perform the four operations, calculate loans, inheritances, etc. and surveyors to calculate the area of agricultural land.

This concept of algorithm is not unique to computing, since it is also used in mathematics, where there are many algorithms for solving equations exactly or approximately, deriving and integrating functional expressions, calculating the probability of certain events, etc. If we start with computing in the 1930s, this concept therefore predates computing. If we start with computing in the 1930s, this concept predates computing, but if we start with mathematics in the 5th century BC, it also predates mathematics. An algorithm is a recipe for solving a certain problem in a systematic way.

A paradigmatic example is the recipe for apple pie, which solves a problem: making an apple pie. However, in this example, it is important to distinguish between the recipe as text and the recipe as practice. A recipe can be executed and even passed down from generation to , without being written down or even verbalised. It is this second notion that corresponds to the notion of algorithm. As soon as the recipe is written or verbalised, it must be compared, not with the notion of algorithm, but with that of programme.

1.2.2. THE MACHINE CONCEPT

For 4,500 years we have been devising algorithms and executing them "by hand", but for the last few we have been using tools to do so. This use tools seems natural, since an algorithm is designed to be executed "without thinking", and this is how, since Antiquity, we have used abacuses - calculating rods, abacuses, chessboards, etc. - and mechanical machines, before we had the technical knowledge to build the tools we needed. - and mechanical machines, before we had the technical knowledge to build today's most common tools: computers.

THE DIVERSITY OF MACHINES

A machine is a tool, i.e. a material system, which therefore obeys the laws of physics. Machines include computers, more specialised devices such as cameras or telephones, and more generally all physical systems for which we have defined an interaction protocol that allows us to exchange data. So we can imagine a machine in which we drop a ball in a vacuum for a period of time t and measure the distance travelled by the ball. This machine performs a special calculation: it squares the number t. The same physical system, equipped with a different protocol, performs another calculation: if we measure the time taken for the ball to travel a distance d, we obtain a machine that calculates the square root of the number d. Today, many machines exploit the physical properties of semiconductors, but there is no reason why this should always be the case and computer science research is exploring many alternatives, in particular by trying to exploit more systematically the possibilities of quantum physics, or to draw inspiration from living processes.

COMPUTING POWER AND THE PRINCIPLES OF PHYSICS

The fact that machines obey the laws of physics limits their power: machines could calculate much more if information could travel instantaneously or if it were possible to store an infinite quantity information in a finite volume.

Less speculatively, the physics of computation establishes a link between the reversibility of a computation, i.e. the possibility of recovering the input values the algorithm from its result, and the reversibility of the evolution of the physical system that performs the computation: when a machine performs an irreversible computation, the physical process itself is irreversible, and therefore dissipates heat. The link between the energy dissipated in the form of heat and the information lost can even be quantified: erasing a bit of information dissipates, in the form of heat, at least an energy $k\ T\ \ln(2)$, where k is Boltzmann's constant, and therefore increases entropy by at least $k \ln(2)$.

SPACE AND NETWORKS

Like any physical system, a machine can have a greater or lesser extension in space, and the desktop computer has gradually been replaced by another, much larger machine, made up of billions of computers interconnected in a network. After the computer, the network is therefore a second instance of this concept of machine, which gives this question of extension in space an essential place. Here we can talk about the "geometry of calculation" when we ask ourselves how to distribute a calculation over different computers located in the four corners of the globe, or how to transmit a message from one point to another.

COMPUTERS

We mentioned two machines, the first of which calculates the square of a number and the second calculates its square root. Each of these machines solves just one problem: calculating a square or calculating a square root. Some multi-purpose machines, such as pocket calculators, can solve several problems: calculating a sum, a difference, a product or a quotient. However, this type of machine can only solve a finite number of problems: even a Swiss army knife only has a finite number of blades.

Hence the old idea of designing machines that can be parameterised, like barrel organs, where you can change the melody, or looms, where you can change the pattern by changing the punched cards.

This evolution has led to universal machines that can execute any algorithm operating on symbolic data, as long as they are equipped with the right "punched cards" and the right program: computers.

PARALLEL AND SPECIALISED MACHINES

However, the construction of universal machines has not completed the history of the There are still many improvements that can be made. In particular, it is possible to group together several machines, either dispersed in various locations and therefore in a network, or located at a few metres from each other, in a grid, or located on the same integrated circuit. When several machines are connected in this way, they can be synchronous, which means that their clocks beat at the same rate, or asynchronous, in which case the execution of all the machines is necessarily non-deterministic, the randomness being introduced by the drift of the clocks, which is unknown.

Other, more specialised machines are used in many telephones, cameras, aircraft, etc. These are known as "on-board systems".

1.2.3. THE CONCEPT OF LANGUAGE

A **computer language** is a language designed to describe the set of consecutive actions that a computer must perform. A computer language is therefore a practical way for us (humans) to give instructions to a computer.

In contrast, the term "natural language" represents the possibilities of expression shared by a group individuals (example, English or French).

The languages used by computers to communicate with each other have nothing to do with computer languages, which are referred to as

communication protocols. A computer language is rigorous:
EACH instruction corresponds to ONE processor action.
The language used by the processor is called **machine language**. This is the data as it arrives at the processor, consisting of a sequence of 0s and 1s (binary data).
This means that machine language cannot be understood by human beings, which is why intermediate languages that can be understood by humans have been developed. Code written in this type of language is transformed into machine language so that it can be used by the processor.
Assembler was the first computer language to used. It is very close to machine language but is still understandable for developers. However, such a language is so close to machine language that it is closely dependent on the type of processor used (each type of processor can have its own machine language). So a programme developed for one machine cannot be *ported* to another type of machine. The term **"portability"** refers to the ability of a computer programme to be used on machines of different types. To be able to use a computer programme written in assembler on another type of machine, it will sometimes be necessary to rewrite the programme entirely!
A computer language has several advantages:

- it is easier to understand than machine language;
- it allows greater portability, i.e. easier adaptation to different types of machine;

IMPERATIVE AND FUNCTIONAL LANGUAGES

There are two main families of programming languages, depending on how instructions are processed:

- imperative languages ;
- functional languages.

IMPERATIVE LANGUAGE

An imperative language organises the programme in the form of a series of instructions, grouped together in blocks and including conditional jumps that allow you to return to a block of instructions if the condition is met. Historically, these were the first languages, although many modern languages still use this operating principle.
However, structured imperative languages suffer from a lack of flexibility due to the sequential nature of the instructions.

FUNCTIONAL LANGUAGE

A **functional language** (sometimes called a *procedural language*) is a language in which the programme is constructed using functions, returning a new state as output and taking the output of other functions as input. When the function calls itself, this is known as recursion.

INTERPRETATION AND COMPILATION

Computer languages can be roughly divided into two categories:

- **interpreted languages**
- **compiled languages**.

INTERPRETED LANGUAGE

A computer language is by definition different from machine language. It must therefore be translated to make it intelligible from the processor's point of view. A program written in an interpreted language needs an auxiliary program (the interpreter) to translate the program instructions as they are written.

COMPILE LANGUAGE

A program written in a language known as "**compiled**" will be translated once and for all by an additional program, called a **compiler**, in order to generate a new file that will be autonomous, i.e. that will no longer need a program other than itself to run; this file is also said to be **executable**.

The advantage of a program written in a compiled language is that, once compiled, no longer needs an additional program to run. In addition, because the translation is done once and for all, it faster to run.

However, it is less flexible than a program written in an interpreted language, because each time the source file (the file that will be compiled) is modified, the program will have to be recompiled for the modifications to take effect.

On the other hand, a compiled programme has the advantage of guaranteeing the security of the source code. In fact, an interpreted language, being directly intelligible (readable), allows anyone to know the manufacturing secrets of a programme and therefore to copy the code or even modify it. There is therefore a risk of copyright infringement. In addition, certain secure applications require confidential code to prevent piracy (banking transactions, online payments, secure communications, etc.).

INTERMEDIATE LANGUAGES

Some languages fall into both categories (LISP, Java, Python, etc.) because programs written in these languages may, under certain conditions, undergo an intermediate compilation phase to produce a file written in a language that is not intelligible (and therefore different from the source file) and not executable (an interpreter is required). Java applets, small programs that are sometimes inserted into web pages, are files that are compiled but can only be run from a web browser (they are files with the .class extension).

SOME EXAMPLES OF COMMONLY USED LANGUAGES

Here is a non-exhaustive list of existing computer languages:

Language	Main area of application	Compiled/interpreted
ADA	Real time	Compiled language
BASIC	Basic programming for educational purposes	Interpreted language
C	System programming	Compiled language
C++	Object system programming	Compiled language
Cobol	Management	Compiled language
Fortran	Calculation	Compiled language
Java	Internet-oriented programming	Intermediate language
MATLAB	Mathematical calculation	Interpreted language
Mathematica	Mathematical calculation	Interpreted language
LISP	Artificial intelligence	Intermediate language
Pascal	Teaching	Compiled language
PHP	Development of websites	Interpreted language
	dynamics	
Prolog	Artificial intelligence	Interpreted language
Perl	Treatment of cams from characters	Interpreted language

1.2.4.CONCEPT INFORMATION

In computing and information technology (IT), the concept of information refers to data that is organised, meaningful and interpretable, processed and stored by computer systems.

In the world of IT, the terms data and information are often used as they were synonyms. But they are not! In fact, the two concepts are very different. Whereas data is a collection of raw facts and figures, information is data that has been processed and contextualised for a user. In this article, discover the sometimes subtle differences between data and information and their definitions.

In an ever-changing digital age, everything is data and everything is information... Understanding the difference between these terms is much more than a semantic subtlety; it's the key to harnessing the full potential of modern technologies. This distinction paves the way for informed decision-making, impactful innovation and skilful navigation in a world saturated with seemingly chaotic data flows.

CHAPTER II

PRESENTATION OF THE COMPUTER

11.1. DEFINITION

A computer is an electronic device capable, by applying predefined instructions (programme), of carrying out automated data processing and interacting with the environment using peripherals (screen, keyboard, etc.).

11.2. TYPE OF COMPUTER

Laptop and desktop computers

- The computers laptops and desktops are from categories computers that differ mainly in their mobility.
- The laptops are designed to be easily desktop computers are designed to remain on a desk.
- Both types of computer have similar components and can perform the same tasks.

Mainframe microcomputers (large computers)

- Mainframe mainframes are powerful computers that centralise the data and processing of an information system.
- They are physically large, measuring several metres in height and width .

- They are capable of storing huge amounts of information, often up to 100 terabytes of hard disk capacity.
- Mainframe mainframes are generally used in large companies or organisations that need to manage large amounts of data.

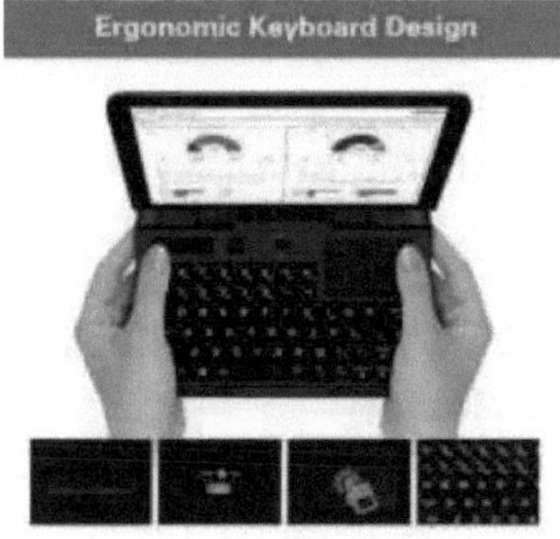

Intermediate (Mini computer, fridge size)

- The category of intermediate computers, such as minicomputers, has disappeared with the evolution of technology.
- These computers were small, comparable in size to a refrigerator, and were used for specific applications.
- However, with the advent of more powerful personal computers, this category of computer was gradually abandoned.

Personal computers (PCs)

- Personal computers, also known as microcomputers or PCs, are small computers designed for use by ordinary people.
- They are equipped a central processing unit consisting one or more microprocessors.
- Personal computers are generally pre-programmed with a set of software and hardware necessary to meet the day-to-day needs of users, such an Internet browser.

Macintosh

- The Macintosh is a brand of personal computer launched in 1984.
- It is known for its user-friendly interface and proprietary operating system.
- Macintosh computers are still in use today and are popular with creative professionals and users who prefer the Apple ecosystem.

Mainframe server (large computer)

- Mainframe servers are powerful computers used to centralise data and processing in large companies.
- They are similar to mainframe mainframes, but are specifically

designed to act as servers in a computer network.

- Mainframe servers are capable of managing large amounts of data and providing services to many users simultaneously.

Server (connected server sheds)

- Servers are computers used to provide services and resources to users on a network.
- They can be grouped together in server sheds, where several servers are connected to form a more powerful system.
- Servers are often located in data centres and are used to host websites, applications and other online services.

PC / Mobile (smartphone/tablet)

- Personal computers and mobile devices such as smartphones and tablets are categories computer used by individual users.
- They are equipped with operating systems such as Android and iOS, which enable them to run variety of applications and services.
- Personal computers and mobile devices have become increasingly popular due to their ease of use and portability.

11.3. COMPUTER GENERATION

FIRST GENERATION: (1945-1955)

"Vacuum tubes and switchboards

In the mid-1940s, "calculation engines" using mechanical relays (cycle times in seconds) were replaced electronic circuits: the vacuum tubes. The result was huge machines that could be programmed by flipping switches or swapping cable connections on a *(plugboard)* .

In the early days, there was language and no operating system.

The first fully electronic digital computer was produced in 1943 under the direction of Thomas FLOWERS in the cryptoanalysis centre at Bletckley Park in England. This machine, the Colossus Mark 1, operated in binary and was programmable. It was used to break German and Japanese ciphers. As with the Turing bomb, the existence of Colossus machines remained a secret until 1975.

In the United States, first electronic computer, 'ENIAC, was developed in secret in 1943 by John Presper ECKERT and John William MAUCHLY at the University of Pennsylvania with the help of mathematician Hermann GOLDSTINE. It was initially designed to calculate artillery firing tables.

ENIAC

The ENIAC was an enormous machine, weighing 30 tonnes and consisting of 18,000 vacuum tubes.

Although the vacuum tube was an electronic type of technology (and not electromechanical like the relay), ENIAC did not adopt the binary calculation principle of the STIBITZ calculator. It operated in decimal. Each digit was coded using a series of 10 vacuum tubes whose name "ring counter" clearly showed that it was an electronic transposition of the cogwheels of the first arithmetic machines.

The plans for ENIAC were completed in 1944 and the machine was inaugurated on 15 February 1946 with a demonstration of a calculation whose programme was written by Adèle Goldstine (At the time, women were considered capable of programming faster and more accurately than men - see The Women of Eniac).

This machine was programmed manually by positioning switches or connecting cables in various configurations. When the programme was complicated, it could take several days.

In 1950, the first improvement was to use punched cards to write programmes.

In 1951, Grace HOPPER designed the first compiler.

In 1954, the Fortran language was the first high-level language to be implemented on a computer.

SECOND GENERATION: (1955-1965)

"Transistors and batch systems

Computers become reliable enough to be produced and sold^ Separation between manufacturers, operators and programmers.

The machines had to be installed in air-conditioned premises, programmed in FORTRAN or assembler via punched cards that the programmers gave to the operators. The operators loaded the programmes into the computer with the compiler if necessary. The results were printed and given to the programmers. ^ These operations were too time-consuming given the size of the investment.

Batch processing :

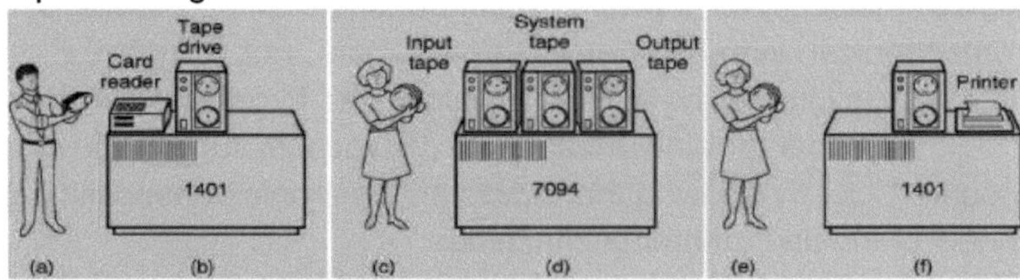

Images from Andrew Tanenbaum's notes

A less expensive machine, such as the IBM 1401, read the cards (a) and copied the code onto a magnetic tape (b). A large computer (IBM 7094) read this tape (c), executed the jobs (d) and then transcribed the results onto another tape (e), thus postponing the printing of the results (off-line printing), which was then done by a lighter computer (f).

The concept of the operating system is emerging.

THE SUCCESSIVE STAGES IN RUNNING A PROGRAMME

- Loading the compiler
- Read the source code and compile it
- Load the executable
- Start execution
- Reading and processing data

In the early 60s, there were two types of computer:

- Those that, like the 7094, were geared towards intensive computing intensive tasks.

The data unit is the word.

- Those with a more commercial purpose, whose data unit is the character (IBM 1401) and which were used by large organisations such as banks and insurance companies to manage magnetic tapes and print data.

^ This resulted in two distinct product lines.

THIRD GENERATION: (1965-1980)

"Integrated circuits - Multiprogramming - Time-sharing

IBM's 360 system, a series of software-compatible machines (same architecture and same instruction set), was designed to suit both scientific and commercial applications.

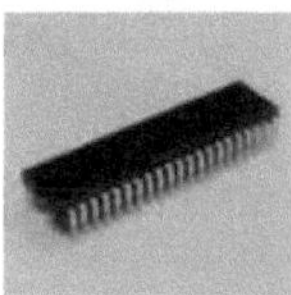

These machines were the first to use integrated circuits, which enabled prices to be cut, and were an immediate success.

This "single family" concept resulted in an OS that had to be as effective on small machines as on large ones, with few or a very large number of peripherals, for commercial or scientific applications^ Huge operating system: Millions of lines of assembler written by thousands of programmers. The result is thousands of bugs!

It was also at this time that the concept of multiprogramming appeared. Memory is shared between different jobs.

When one of them is waiting for an I/O to be performed, another job can take over the CPU. ^ The utilisation rate is close to 100%.

Another new feature is SPOOL: *Simultaneous Peripheral Operation On Line*.

This is the ability given to applications to simultaneously share the same slow device (printer, card reader, etc.). In the case of a printer, the print stores the documents to be printed and sends them one after the other for printing.

Problem! Impossibility of following the programme as it runs to fine-tune it^ Time-sharing : several users = each has an online terminal.

At the time, it was imagined that computers would become huge machines providing computing power to hundreds of users: the MULTICS (*Multiplexed Information and Computing Service*)

The IBM 360 computer, shown in a promotional photo from 1964

It was also the time of the breakthrough of minicomputers such as the DEC PDP-1 in 1961.

The PDP-1 had 4k 18-bit words for $120,000 (5% of the price of an IBM 7094). It was followed by others up to the PDP-11.

It was on a PDP-7 that Ken Thompson began writing a single-user version of **MULTICS**, which served as the basis for the **UNIX** system.

The UNIX source code was published and developed in several versions (incompatible)

The IEEE has developed a standard called **POSIX**, to which most current versions of UNIX (and other systems) conform.

In 1987, Andrew TANENBAUM developed **MINIX**, a small UNIX clone for educational purposes. educational purposes.

Linus Torvald has released a production version: **LINUX**

NB. The notes in this chapter owe a great deal to the excellent teacher Andrew Tannebaum, whose personal website can .be found here

FOURTH GENERATION (1980 - . . .)

"Thousands, ... millions of transistors on a chip".

LSI circuits - *Large Scale Integration circuits* containing thousands of transistors per mm(2) - were developed in the mid-1970s for the first microprocessors. They enabled the manufacture of what were known as microcomputers or personal . computersThey were not very different from the PDP-11 except for the price^ an individual can own his own machine: the PC = Personal Computer.

Today, we no longer talk about LSI circuits. At the end of the 70s, they replaced by **VLSI** - *Very Large Scale Integration*: several hundred thousand transistors.

During the 1980s, integrated circuit integration became ultra-large scale **ULSI** - *Ultra Large Scale Integration*: millions of transistors on a single chip.

Each year, the engraving of the circuits becomes finer and the scale integration larger.

CHAPTER III

BASIC COMPUTER PERIPHERALS

111.1. PROCESSOR

The **processor**, or **CPU** (*Central Processing* Unit), is the computer component that runs the computer programs. Along with memory, it is one of the components that has existed since the first computers and is present in all computers. A processor built into a single integrated circuit is called a microprocessor.

The invention of the transistor in 1948 paved the way for the miniaturisation of electronic components.

Early processors were designed specifically for a given type of computer. This costly method of designing processors for a specific application led to the development of mass production of processors suitable for one or more uses. This trend towards standardisation, which began with mainframe computers (discrete transistor *mainframes* and minicomputers), accelerated rapidly with the advent of integrated circuits. Integrated circuits have enabled the miniaturisation of processors. The miniaturisation and standardisation of processors has led to their widespread use in modern life well beyond the uses of dedicated programmable machines.

COMPOSITION OF A PROCESSOR

The essential parts of a processor are :

- the *and* **Logic Unit** (UAL), which is responsible for *Logical Unit* (*ALU*), which performs basic arithmetic calculations and tests;
- the **control unit** or **sequencer**, which synchronises the various elements of the processor. In particular, it initialises the registers when the machine and sets the interrupts;
- **registers**, whichare small small size (a few bytes), fast enough for the ALU to manipulate their contents with each clock cycle. A number of registers are common to most processors:
  - **Ordinal counter**: this register contains the memory address of the instruction in progress ;
  - **accumulator**: this register is used to store data currently being processed by the UAL ;
  - **address** : this contains the address of the next information to be read by the UAL, either the continuation of current instruction or the next instruction;
  - **Instruction** : contains the instruction currently being processed;

- **status register**: this is used to store the processor context, which means that the various bits in this register are flags (*flags*) used to store information about the result of the last instruction executed;
- **stack pointers**: this type of register, the number of which varies depending on the type of processor, contains the address of the top of the stack (or stacks);
- **general registers**: these registers are available for calculations ;

- the **clock** which synchronises all the actions of the CPU. It is present in synchronous processors, and absent from asynchronous processors and auto-synchronous processors;
- the **input-output unit**, which handles communication with the computer's memory or the transmission of orders to drive its specialised processors, enabling the processor to access the computer's peripherals.

Today's processors also incorporate more complex elements:

- several ALUs, enabling several instructions to be processed at the same time **Superscalar architecture**, in particular, allows the ALUs to be arranged in parallel, with each ALU able to execute an instruction independently of the other;
- **Pipeline architecture** enables the processing to be split up in time. This technique comes from the world of supercomputers;
- a **jump prediction unit**, which enables the processor to anticipate a jump in the flow of a program, thus avoiding waiting for the definitive address value of the jump. This allows the pipeline to be filled more efficiently;
- **a** *Floating Point Unit* (*FPU*), which accelerates calculations on real numbers encoded in floating point format;
- **cache memory**, which speeds up processing by reducing memory access times. These buffers are much faster than RAM and slow down the CPU less. The instruction cache receives the next instructions to be executed, while the data cache handles the data. Sometimes a single unified cache is used for both code and data. Several levels of caches can coexist, often referred to as L1, L2 or L3. In advanced processors, special units of the processor are dedicated to the search, using statistical and/or predictive means, for the next central memory accesses.

A processor is defined by :

- the width of its internal data manipulation registers (8, 16, 32, 64, 128) bits;
- its clock rate expressed in MHz (mega hertz) or GHz (giga hertz);

- the number of calculation cores ;
- its instruction set *architecture* (*ISA*), which depends on the family (CISC, RISC, etc.);
- its engraving fineness expressed in nm (nanometres) and its microarchitecture.

But the main characteristic of a processor is the family to which it belongs:

- CISC (Complex Instruction Set Computer: choice of instructions as close as possible to a high-level language) ;
- RISC (Reduced Instruction Set Computer: choice of simpler instructions and a structure allowing very fast execution);
- VLIW (Very Long Instruction Word) ;
- DSP (Digital Signal Processor). Although this last family (DSP) is relatively specific. A processor is in fact a programmable component and is therefore *a priori* capable of running any type of programme. However, in the interests of optimisation, specialised processors are designed and adapted to certain types of calculation (3D, sound, etc.). DSPs are specialised processors for signal processing calculations. For example, it is not uncommon to see Fourier Transforms implemented in a DSP.

A processor has three types of bus:

- a **data bus**, defines the size of the data that can be manipulated (regardless of the size of the internal registers) ;
- an **address bus** defines the number of memory cells accessible ;
- a **control bus** defines the management of the IRQ processor, RESET, etc.

111.2. MEMORIES

There are currently four types of computer memory, all of which are present in a computer. These can be grouped into two distinct categories: **non-volatile memory**, which includes **ROM** and **flash memory**, and **volatile memory**, which includes **RAM** and **cache memory**. Let's take a closer look at these forms of memory and how they work.

A.ROM

Read-only memory (or ROM = *Read Only Memory*) is a **non-volatile** computer memory that can be compared to a **computer's hard drive**. Its contents are fixed when it is programmed, and can be read several times by the user, but can no longer be modified. Once the information is recorded in the computer, it remains **stored** for **several years**. What's more, when it comes to accessing its contents, it is much **slower** than random access memory, which we'll look at next. It generally stores the information needed to **initialise** the device (boot system), i.e. the operating system such as Windows.

The access time to read-only memory is of the order of **150 nanoseconds**, compared with an access time of around 10 nanoseconds for random access memory. To speed up data processing, data stored in ROM is generally copied to RAM before being processed. This operation is known as **shadowing**.

This non-volatile memory includes **magnetic memory**. It can have a very **large** storage **capacity**. Both internal and external hard disks work with this type of memory. Hard disks are found in many of today' devices, such as **games consoles** and **telephones**. This magnetic memory works by means of tiny magnetisable zones that are magnetically oriented to the north or south of the **electromagnet**. It is thanks to these magnets that we are able to create hard disks and other devices with ever higher densities and ever smaller sizes.

B.RAM

Random Access Memory (**RAM**) is a **volatile memory** that much **faster** to access than non-volatile memory. It enables the device to function properly by **storing** the **necessary information**. In fact, there are several data locations in this memory, which can access one of these locations by means of an address. RAM is readable by the computer and can even be completely **rewritten**, but the information in this type of memory **disappears** once the computer is switched off.

There are two sub-types of volatile memory. There is **static memory** (SRAM, *Static Random Access Memory*), which contains all the information that only disappears once the computer **has been switched**

off. For example, if you are writing a text on Microsoft Word and there is a power cut, when you turn the computer back on, the text you have typed cannot be retrieved unless it has been saved on the hard disk. The advantage of this static memory is that there is no need to **refresh** it, as the information remains as it is.

The other sub-type is **Dynamic** *RAM* (DRAM), which is **denser** than static memory. It can hold more information than static memory in a smaller volume, but the information it contains is lost after a few **milliseconds**. In fact, the computer must constantly **reread** this information and, once it has been read, **modify** it so it remains reliable. This is a very labour-intensive operation, but as the digital memory is organised like a table, the computer modifies it line by line, very **quickly**.

The most common hardware for this type of memory is the **RAM strip**. These are printed circuits that are widely used in computers. These memories are very fast, but of low capacity.

C.FLASH MEMORY

Flash memory is **a compromise** between **RAM** and **ROM**: it is a non-volatile memory, like read-only memory, but it also has the characteristics of random access memory. **It can be accessed** very **quickly** and **is rewritable**. Its contents can be erased very easily. However, the data it contains does not disappear when the computer is switched off: it is a **non-volatile** memory. Flash memory stores data bits in memory cells that are retained when the power supply is switched off.

Its **high speed**, **long life** and **low power consumption** (which is even zero when idle) make it very useful for a wide range of applications: digital cameras, mobile phones, printers, laptops or sound playback and recording devices such as portable players, USB sticks, etc.

D. THE HIDDEN MEMORY

The cache memory is a **volatile memory** built into a computer's **processor** (the element that calculates the information stored in RAM). It only stores data for a very short time. The aim is to make the operations linked to this memory very fast. It gives the processor rapid access to the most useful data and instructions. It saves the processor from having to **go back and forth** to RAM all the time.

However, the cost is **high** and the storage capacity remains relatively **low**. It is only used within a single component to store the result of a calculation, for example.

111.3. DISCS

A hard disk is an internal or external computer component that stores data, such as the operating system, applications and user files.

Hard disks are "non-volatile" storage devices, meaning that they retain stored data even when the computer is not running.

HARD DRIVE OPERATION

A hard disk has two main components: a turntable and a mechanical arm.

- The **platter** is a circular magnetic disc containing tracks and sectors for storing data.

- The **mechanical arm** moves across the platter to read and write the data.

The platter rotates (hence the name) on a spindle to speed up the read/write process as the mechanical arm moves over it.
The data sectors are distributed randomly (known as "fragmented") across the platter, and we'll look below at how to defragment a hard disk to boost its performance.

WHAT DOES A HARD DRIVE LOOK LIKE?

The platter and arm are delicate physical mechanisms. A solid casing covers them to prevent damage during normal use. The hard drive protection looks like a metal case. It is clearly identified as a hard drive.
This is what an internal hard drive looks like under its metal casing. You can see the turntable and the mechanical arm, and how they work together to read and write data on demand.

Instead of a hard disk, the most recent computers are generally equipped with a SSD.

THE ADVANTAGES AND DISADVANTAGES OF A HARD DRIVE

BENEFITS	DISADVANTAGES
• Hard disks can store a large amount of data (this varies depending on the size of the disk). • They are relatively inexpensive compared to other storage solutions	• Hard disks can be slow to recover large files • They consume more energy • Moving parts generate a lot of heat • They are less durable, particularly in portable devices

111.4. INPUT UNITS

The input unit of a computer refers to **the input device and part of the**

computer hardware that is used to transport data. The data processing system involves the computer's information devices with the computer's control and data signals. Example: mouse, camera and keyboard.

111.5. OUTPUT UNITS

The output unit: The computer output unit **is the peripheral that manages the transmission of computer data between the device and clients**. The computer is designed for humans in audio and video format. Examples include monitors, printers, microphones and headphones.

CHAPTER IV

THE BASIC COMPONENTS OF A COMPUTER

111.6. CRAN

A screen or **monitor** is the usual output device of a computer. It is the **screen** on which information entered or requested by the user and generated or output by the computer , is displayedin the form of text and two-dimensional images, possibly with a three-dimensional effect. Text and images can be fixed or animated.

On some systems, the screen can also be used as an input device: the user can choose an action by touching the corresponding part of the screen, if the system so provides; this is referred to as a touch screen.

Technologies

There are various technologies available:

- cathode ray tube (or CRT) screens, which have the widest viewing angle and, until 2005, the best colour rendering, but they are heavy, bulky and energy-hungry ,
- liquid crystal displays (or LCDs), which are light and convenient, but have poorer colour rendition and, in the case of some entry-level models, a persistence that can be annoying for very fast games or animations (films, etc.).
- plasma screens, with very good rendering, but expensive and with a more limited lifespan ,
- DLP (Digital Light Processing) with millions of mirrors,
- SED (Surface-conduction Electron-emitter Display) screens, not yet on the market, were due to arrive at the end of 2006/beginning of 2007 (postponed for an unknown date); they use a mini-cathode tube for each pixel; the rendering is very close to CRT screens, for a comparable thickness and a price similar to LCD screens.

IV.2.KEYBOARD

A computer keyboard is an input device used to enter characters and to communicate instructions to the computer.

The keyboard generally has around a hundred keys representing the different characters of the alphabet, numbers from 0 to 9, and special characters (accented characters, punctuation, etc.).

the keyboard has become a fantastic gateway to the computer's many functions, not least the Internet!

Here's a look at the **main types of keyboard** and **their history**.

A LITTLE HISTORY

The first **computer keyboards** were developed around 1960, modelled on **typewriter** keyboards!

The original **layout of the keys** was designed to **prevent the typewriter stems of** the time **from crossing and jamming**.

The **letters** most commonly used in the **English language** are distributed in such a way **as to be as far apart as possible**.

Successive additions have been **made** to the **keyboard**, including the **numeric keypad**, **function keys** and **multimedia keys**.

THE MAIN TYPES OF KEYBOARD

The **layout of the keys** depends on the **country** and the **language used**. The 2 **most popular key layouts** are: the **AZERTY** keyboard, used in France and Belgium, and the **QWERTY** keyboard, designed for English, a language that is written without accents.

The **Azerty** keyboard :

The **Qwerty** keyboard :

Note: these different keyboards take their name from the layout of the **first six letters** of **the first** row of alphabetic keys.

HOW TO CONNECT A KEYBOARD

A **keyboard** can be connected either by **cable** or **Bluetooth**

KEYBOARD USER PROFILES

Keyboard users can be divided into 3 categories:

- experienced **typists**: who **have mastered the art of keyboarding** with both hands, their ten fingers, without even looking at the keys, and all at a disconcerting speed.
- the "**imposters**": these are **the people who type quickly** (often loudly) **but with 2 or 3 fingers**. This is the majority us.
- the "**slightly lost**" who discreetly ask their neighbour how to write "@" or a €.

IV.3.MICE

The mouse was invented in 1963, but did not become the standard pointing device until the 1980s.

What's the mouse for?

The mouse is an input device. More precisely, it is a pointing device.

The mouse is an electronic extension of the user's finger, controlling the cursor movements by its own movements activated manually by the

user. These movements are read by the optical reader and converted into signals telling the computer how the mouse is moving. On the screen, the cursor moves in the same direction as the mouse on the carpet.
Depending on the action, the cursor changes appearance: how do you use it?
The 4 main mouse manoeuvres

- the click,
- double-click,
- click and drag
- right-click.

Animated illustration : Move the cursor over the mouse...
The essentials
The mouse is an essential input device for computer to work properly.
The cursor is used to select files or documents, or to move the cursor from one point to another on the screen.

CHAPTER V

FUNDAMENTALS OF WINDOWS

V.1.ICONS

The icons are pictograms that you come across very regularly on Windows. An icon represents either a folder, or a software, or a file. ...

Various icons in Windows

You need to double-click on it to access its contents. Double-clicking means clicking twice very quickly (and without moving the mouse) with the left mouse button. Icons can take any shape and we will learn to recognise them easily.

There are 4 main families of 'icons which we will look at in detail in a moment.

Here's a Windows screen dotted with icons:

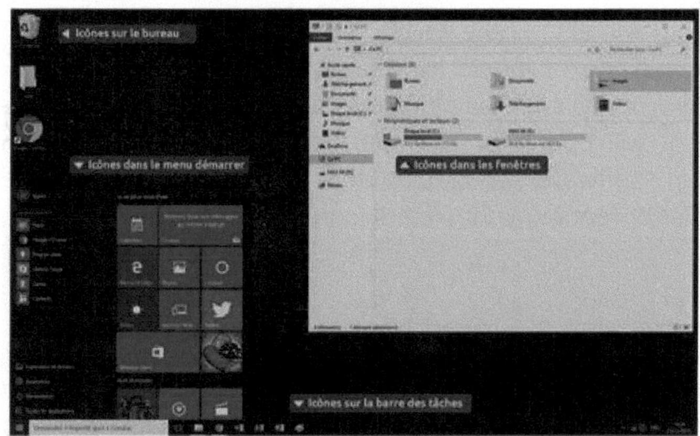

Icons everywhere!

1. THE DIFFERENT TYPES OF ICON

We are now going to take a look at the 4 families of 'icons' that coexist on Windows. For most of them, it will be easy to draw an analogy with the real world, in order to understand them better.

1.1 FILES

Definition

A file is a record of computer data stored on your computer. It can represent music, a film, a text document, a table, etc. Each file is represented visually by an icon.

Windows will automatically display a icon according to the type of file it represents, i.e. all music will have the same pictogram, all text documents another pictogram and so on. So you know at a glance whether your file is a photo, a piece of music or a document.

Some different types of icons: Text documents, music, images...

Your system will also know which software to use to launch this file. If you open a piece of music by double-clicking on it, the music-playing software will open, such as **Windows Media Player**. If you open a text document it will open, for example, with Microsoft Office Word (word processing) software.
Depending on the software that will be responsible for reading your file, its icon may vary. For example :

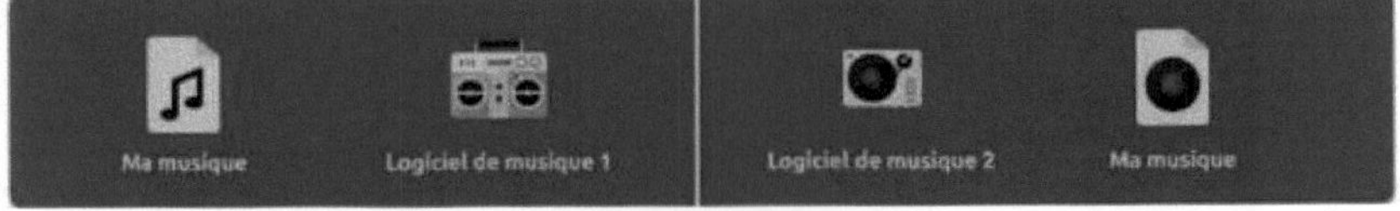

A file's icon may vary depending on the software used to open it

In the case on the left, the chosen music software displays a file containing a musical note, on the right, the default software shows a vinyl on the icon.

Exception: For photos, videos and music (and sometimes other files) , the standard ' icon will be replaced by a preview of the image in question, album cover or film image, which is visually easier to find!
NB: If no software can read the type of file you trying to open, Windows will warn you that it cannot open the file. You will therefore need to install the appropriate software. The hardest part is knowing which software can open the type of file.

1.2 DOSSIERS

The purpose of folders, as in the real world, is to store our files.

Definition

A folder has exactly the same function as in the real world: to store files and other information. Folders are generally represented in yellow on Windows, have a name and can contain an infinite amount of data.
You can create as many folders as you like. The storage and organisation of your files is the subject of a whole section of this course, which I'll save for later.

What can be stored in a folder?

You'll be able to store everything! Films, music, invoices, quotes, e-mails and even other files ! Files within files? Yes! In real life, we store our folders in cupboards, which are themselves in desks. On Windows, we cascade folders. Does that sound a bit vague? You'll see, it's really quite simple, just look at the diagram below:

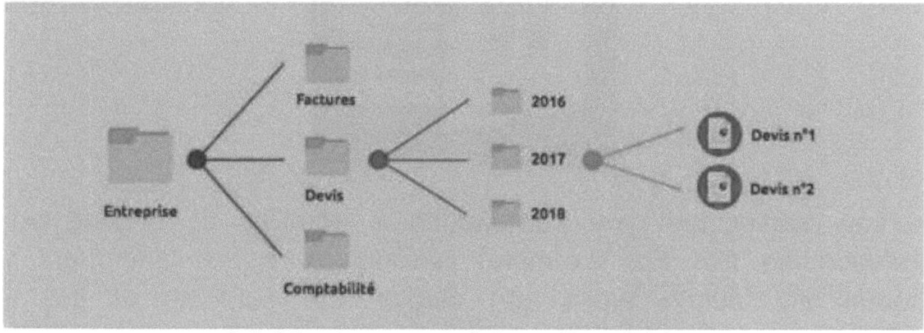

A folder tree containing other folders

This is an example of how to organise company documents: basically, we have a company file. Within this folder, each subfolder has a specific function: quotes, invoices, accounts, projects, etc. Within the quotes folder, each subfolder represents a year: 2016, 2017, 2018.
This is just an example, but it's an easy way to find a file! You can imagine the same concept for organising your music: first by genre, then by artist and finally by album! Don't worry, we'll learn all about that soon enough!

1.3 PROGRAMMES & SOFTWARE

1.3.1.1.SOFTWARE

Definition

Software is a programme that provides the computer with a set of additional functions that are not necessarily present at the outset. Software is installed on the computer via a disc (CD, DVD) or by downloading it from the Internet. Some software is free and some has to be paid for.

We saw earlier that you can launch a program by clicking on a corresponding file. For example, clicking on a text document will automatically launch Word and display the contents of the file. Consequently, it is only useful to launch a program when you want to create a new file.

1.4 THE RACCOURCIS

Programs are actually installed in Windows and are not accessible to the user. A program needs a whole bunch of complex things to work and is therefore installed in a specific place that is not easily accessible to the public.

That's where the shortcuts come in!

1.5 .RACCOURCI

Definition

A shortcut is an icon that can be placed anywhere to provide quick access to a program or area of the computer. It is a shortcut that is most often used to launch a programme. Deleting a shortcut does not uninstall the programme it leads to!

The shortcuts are easy to recognise: they always have a little arrow in a square at the bottom left of the ' icon!

NB: A shortcut takes you quickly to a program but is not the program itself. So if you delete a shortcut, you are not uninstalling the programme that goes with it, just your shortcut icon!

To summarise

Here are the 4 types of icon you will come across on Windows :

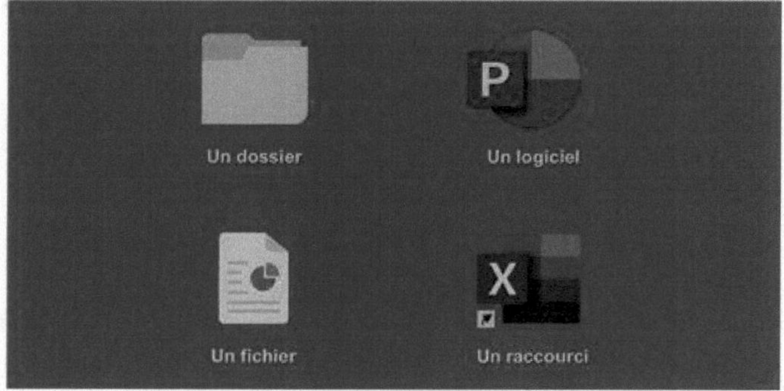

The 4 types of Windows icon: Folders, Software, Files and Shortcuts

V.2.OFFICE

1. What is the Windows desktop?

When you start up the computer, after **logging in**, you place **your documents** (letters, invoices, books, etc.) and **tools** (scissors, tape, rulers, pencils, etc.) **that you often use** on a **real desk** (made of wood or metal).

And your **desk** may be **tidy** or **sometimes very untidy** because you pile up **too many things** on it **that aren't often used**.

In the same way, the **Windows desktop** is used to **store the things you use often.** Here**,** the things **to put** on the **desktop** are **documents** (files, images, folders, etc.) **and tools (**applications**).**

Documents and **applications** are represented on the **Windows desktop** in the form of **icons** set against a **background image**, also known as the **screen background**.
An **icon** is a small **pictogram** (image) representing a **file**, **application** or **folder**. In fact, the **icon** is a **shortcut** (i.e. a link) to the **resource** (file, application) **stored** on **the hard disk**.
Icons make the Windows **graphical interface** easier to use, as you simply click (left-click once) on the **icon** to open it.
Some examples of **icons** representing the **recycle bin**, **folder** and the main **file types** :

Some examples of **icons** representing the most popular **applications**:

Note: when you remove an icon from the desktop, this does **not delete** the **file** or **application** stored on the hard disk!
NB: take the time to arrange the icons on your desktop so that you can see them more clearly!
Put only the documents and applications you use **often** on it

CUSTOMISING A WINDOWS DESKTOP

Windows lets you customise your desktop. Let's find out how!

CHANGE THE THE SIZE OF DESKTOP ICONS WINDOWS

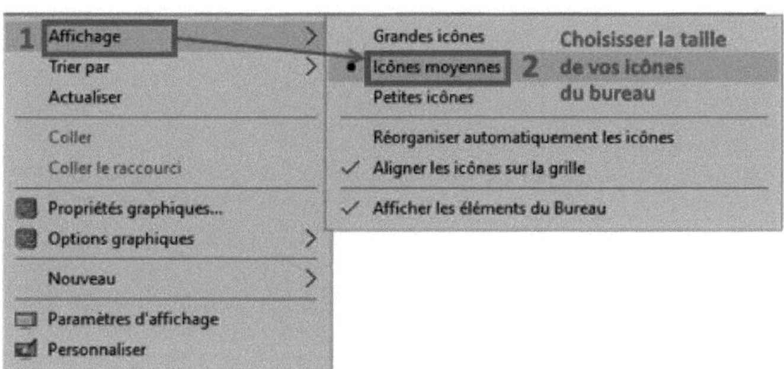

To change the size of your desktop icons, **right-click** anywhere on your

desktop image:
1. click on the **View** option
2. then click on **Large icons, Medium icons** or **Small icons**

SORTING AND ARRANGING WINDOWS DESKTOP ICONS

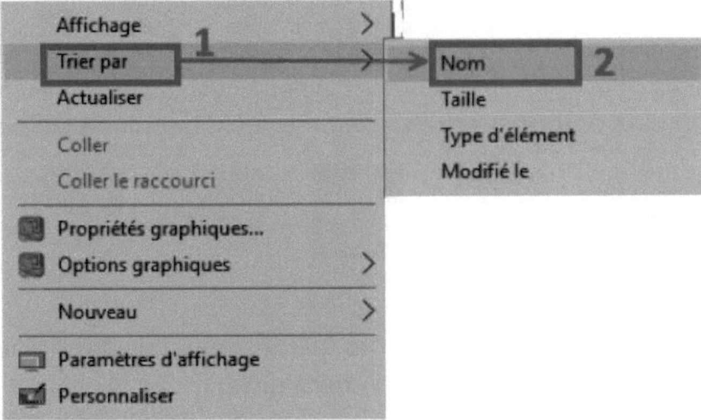

To sort your desktop **icons automatically**, **right-click** anywhere on your desktop image:
1. click on the **Sort by** option
2. then click on **Name, Size, Item type** or **Modified on**

You can also **manually move each icon** on the desktop by **left-clicking** on the **icon you want to move** and then **dragging it with the mouse** to the desired location.

CHANGE THE BACKGROUND IMAGE OF THE WINDOWS DESKTOP

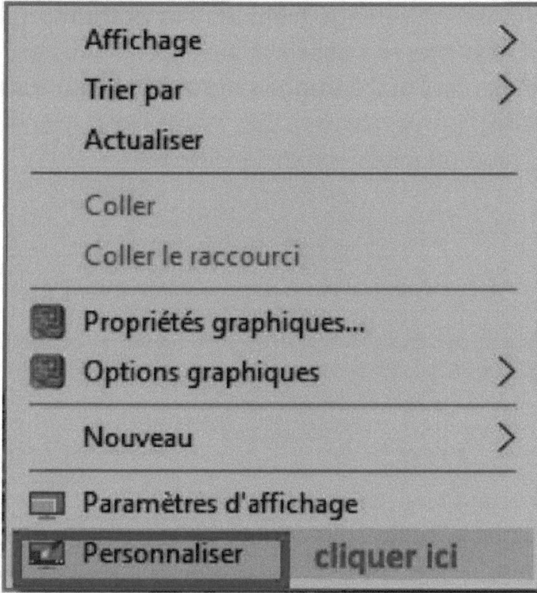

To change **desktop background image**, **right-click** anywhere on the current desktop image:

1. then click on the **Customise** option

The following screen appears:

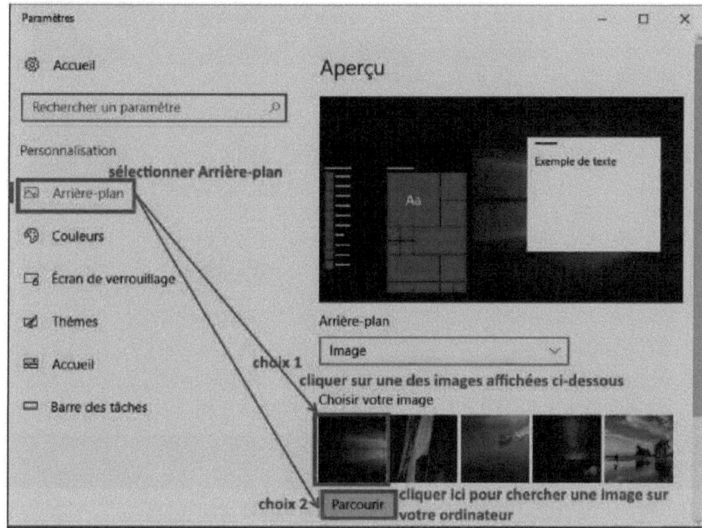

*Select the **Background** option, then*

1. **choice 1**: choose your **image from** the **list of thumbnail images**
2. **choice 2**: if you are not satisfied with these images, browse your computer to choose one of the **images stored on your hard drive.**

V .3 WINDOWS

As soon as you click on a icon, opens a window.

DEFINITION

A window is a rectangular area that appears on the screen to display the contents of a folder or software program. The window can take up all the space (full screen) or just part of it. All graphical system interfaces use windows. It is possible to display and cascade several windows simultaneously and drag items from one to another.

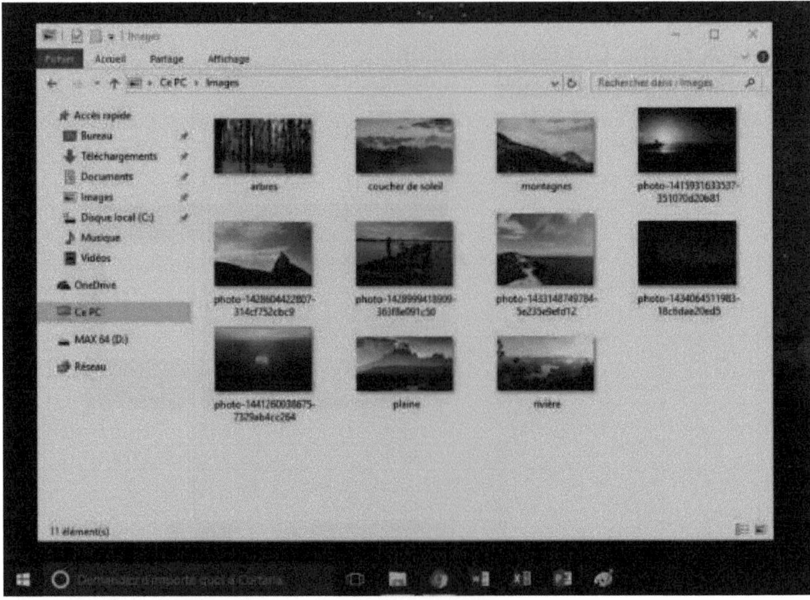

Open a folder display its contents in a window

A window opens when you double-click on a folder or open a program. It

is used to display and delimit its contents. The principle is that several windows can be displayed at the same time on the screen.
When a window is open in Windows, its icon appears in the taskbar at the bottom of the screen. You can switch from one open window to another by clicking on the corresponding icon.

Windows and their indicators

We are now going to take a window apart:

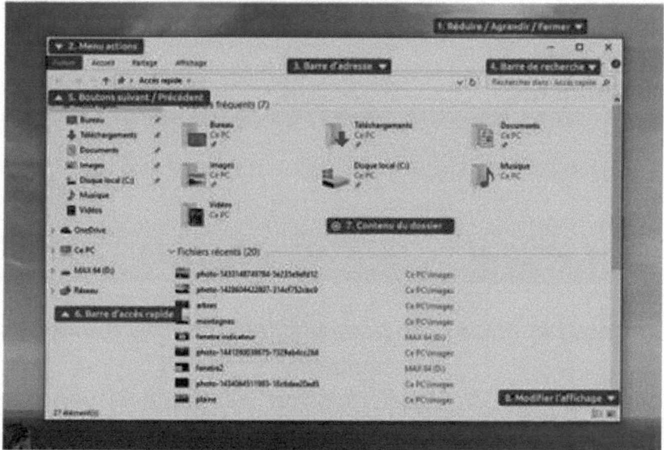

A window and its various elements in Windows 7

REDUCE, ENLARGE AND CLOSE BUTTONS

These 3 buttons are very important and will be omnipresent on all Windows windows and software.

Minimise button: represented by a horizontal line, this button removes the window from the screen but does not close it. It is always present in the taskbar, at the bottom of the screen, so you can display it again later without having to go back and find the corresponding folder.

Enlarge/Restore button: represented by a square, this button allows you to make your window full screen, so that you can view the contents of the folder more easily. Clicking it again will restore the window to its original size.

Close button: represented by a cross, this button closes the window or the software. We will be using it very regularly. When you are in a program and you click on this close button, you may be asked if you want to save your work first before quitting, so as not to lose any unsaved data.

ACTION MENU

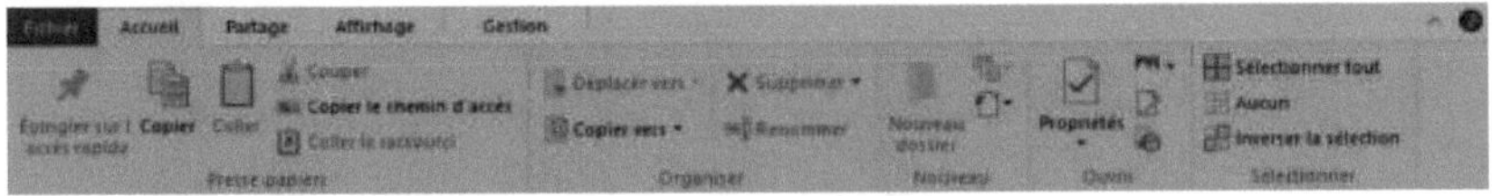

The window menu offers a wide range of actions

This menu adapts automatically to offer you functions related to the contents of your folder: if you have images, Windows will suggest that you print them, if you have music, it will suggest that you listen to it...

For the time being, we won't need go into these menus, but if you're curious, take a look!

THE ADDRESS BAR

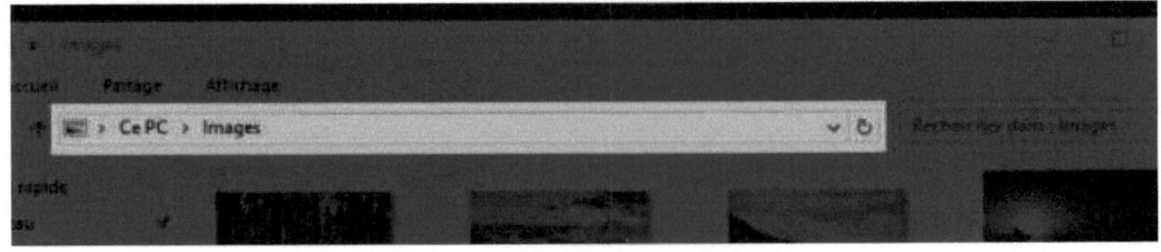

The address bar shows the user which folder they are currently in currently

Once we've mastered Windows, this bar will come in very handy as it tells you where you are on your computer at the moment (a bit like a GPS). It allows you to see at a glance who your parent folders are.

RESEARCH

The search bar for easily finding a file lost in a folder

This handy search field lets you quickly find a file by typing part of its name or content. The results will then be displayed in zone 7.

NEXT / PREVIOUS BUTTONS

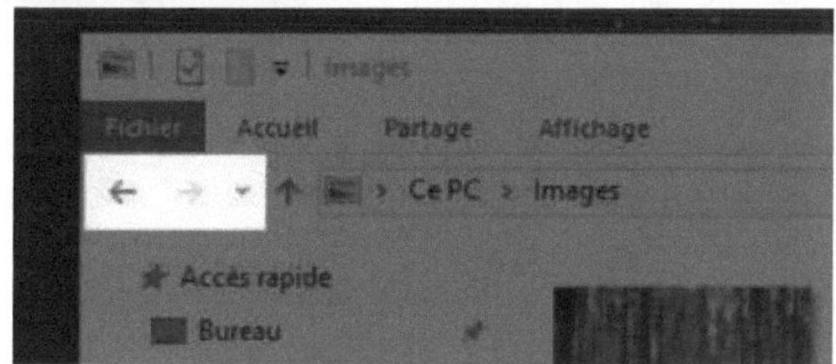

NAVIGATION ARROWS

The first two arrows allow you to navigate between folders. In other words, if you are in a folder and want to return to the previously visited folder, simply click on the **Back** arrow: the one pointing to the left.

THE QUICK ACCESS BAR

Located on the left of the window, this pane lists the various important Windows locations: your personal documents (images, videos, documents, downloads), USB keys, disks, the network, etc. This will be the subject of a later chapter. This **is an important** area that will enable us to navigate quickly through our personal data.

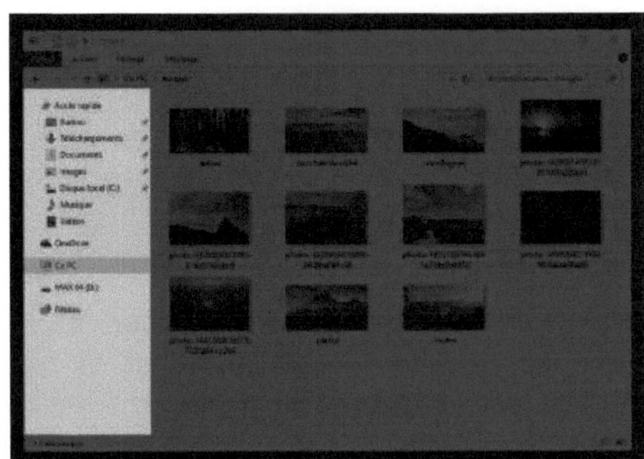

The quick access bar takes you everywhere

THE CONTENTS OF THE FILE

The largest area of the window displays the contents of the folder you have opened: in this case there are several sub-folders (one for music, one for photos, one for films, etc.).

This is the most important area of the window, as it displays what you are looking for: files and folders.

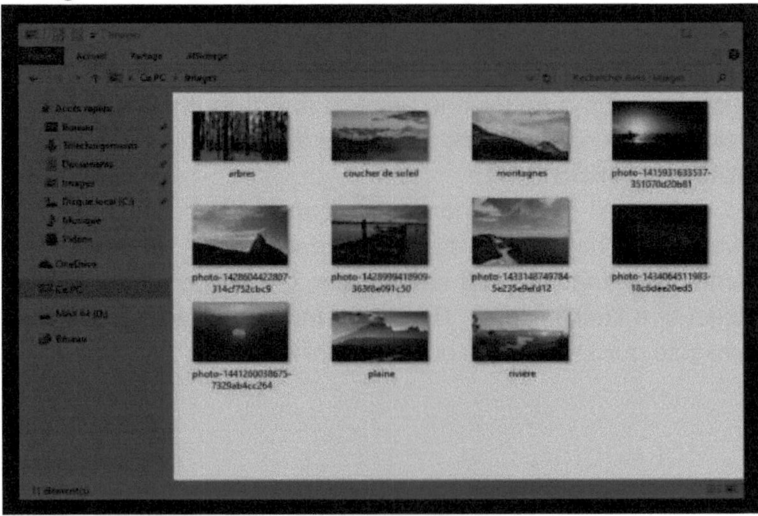

This area displays the files in the folder. In this case, photos.

DISPLAY MODES

This is a very practical tool, as it allows you display your window in different ways: with large thumbnails if it's an image, or as a table if it's a file.

CHANGING THE DISPLAY OF A WINDOW

For each folder, you can choose the display you find most convenient: large, small icons, list, detail...

Try and find the display that suits you best for each folder depending on the type of file :

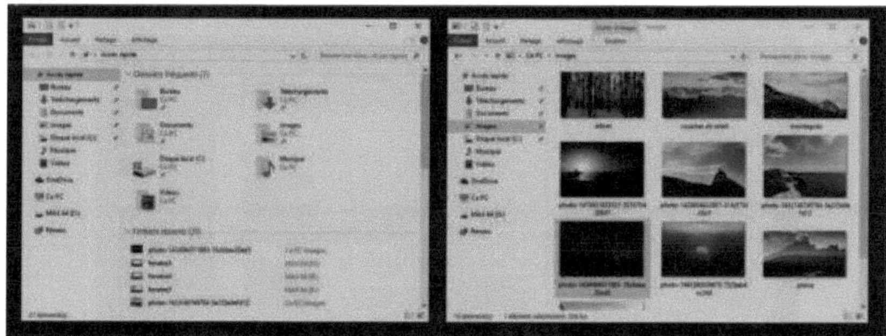

Left: view by folder and list. Right: thumbnail view

RESIZING AND MOVING A WINDOW

A window can be resized (if it is not full screen) and even moved.

TO MOVE THE WINDOW

The easiest way to do this is to place your cursor on the top area of the window, as shown in the image below, then click and hold down the mouse button. Move your mouse: the window follows the cursor! Then release the button.

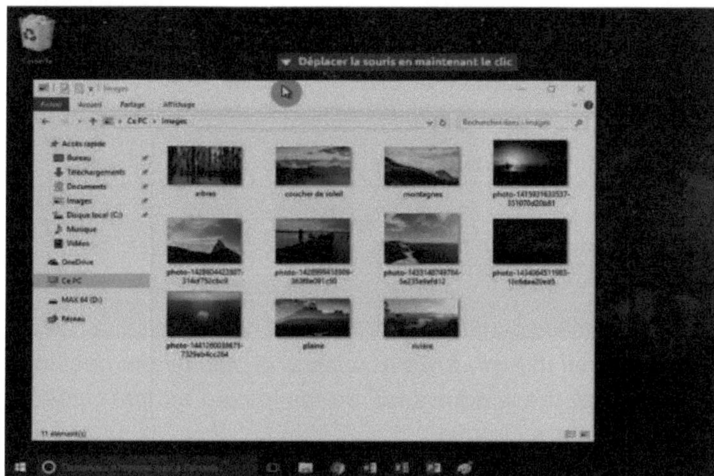

Moving a window

TO RESIZE THE WINDOW

This time you need to move the cursor either to the edge of the window or to a corner. When you are in the right place, the cursor changes appearance and becomes a double arrow. All you have to do then is click and hold, while moving the mouse in the desired direction. Release the pressure to apply!

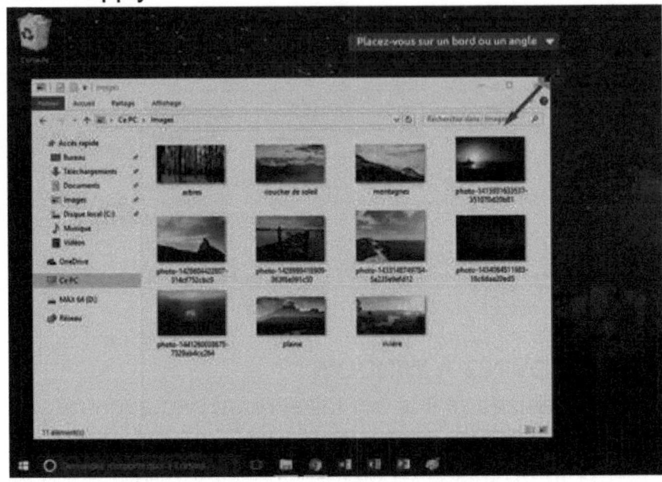

Resizing a Windows window

REDUCE ALL THE WINDOWS AT THE SAME TIME

If you keep opening windows, you can't see the desktop behind them. To avoid closing windows one by one to find the desktop and having to reopen them later, there is a icon, at the bottom right of the screen on Windows 7 and 10.

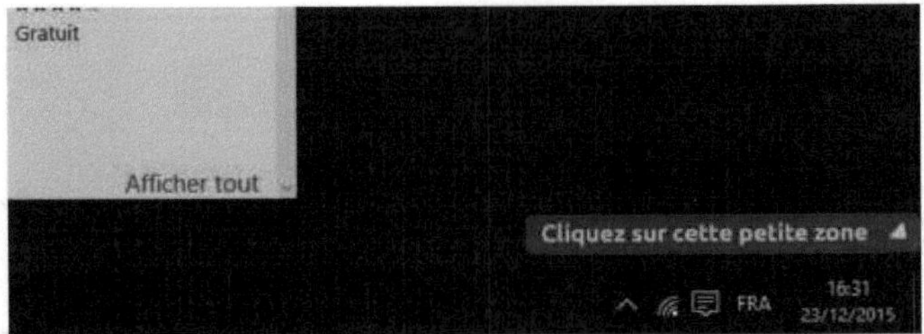

Minimise all the windows at once and display the desktop

By clicking on it, all the windows will be minimised but not closed. Handy for seeing things more clearly!

TIP

To stay organised, try not to overload your computer by opening too many windows. Keep only the most useful ones open . This will you see

things more clearly and not slow down your computer.
That's it! Another completed course! A bit long, but windows are an essential part of understanding Windows. Let's move on to screens!

CHAPTER VI

FILES AND DIRECTORIES

VI .1.FILE FORMAT

A file is an organised collection of information, designated by a specific name, which a computer's operating system handles as a single entity, in its memory or on a storage medium.

The file format influences the accessibility of the file content and the long-term storage of that content, as software and data storage technology evolve rapidly and files can easily become obsolete or difficult access.

It is therefore essential to think about the initial format of the data and the formats used for storage, as it is possible to convert files from one format to another, but this may result in loss of information.

There are two families of file formats: open formats and closed or proprietary formats.

1. **Open format (free format)**

It is independent of any specific software. It is therefore preferable for a access to public and for longevity.

It increase your ability to open and read your files in the long term and make your data usable and accessible to more researchers immediately.

2. **Closed format (proprietary format)**

Linked to specific software from a supplier, which must be used to read the file and modify it. File specifications are not freely available, so when the software is no longer supported, files in this format are generally unreadable.

EXAMPLES OF OPEN FORMATS :

- Database: XML, CSV
- Image: JPG, PNG, PDF, TIFF, BMP
- Sound: MP3, FLAC
- Text: TXT, CSV, PDF/A, ASCII, UTF-8
- Video : MPG, MOV, AVI
- Spreadsheet: CSV
- Medical imaging: DICOM

VI.2.FILE SIZE

In computing, file size is a **measure of the amount of data contained in a computer file or, alternatively, the amount of storage it consumes**. Generally, the size of the file is expressed in units of measurement based on the byte.

The **unit of measurement** in **computing** is the byte. It has several variants, including **Megabytes** and **Gigabytes**, which are the respective definitions of the acronyms **MB and GB**. These are computer storage capacities used to measure the weight of a digital file or peripheral. In other words, when you want to assess the size of a file, image, video or audio on a **computing device** (computer, smartphone, tablet, external hard drive, **USB stick, etc**.), you need to ask about its storage capacity in MB, GB or other units. Video files are often stored in MB or GB.

THE LARGER SIZE OF COMPUTER FILES

The largest **computer file size** is the yottabyte (Yo). This is a unit of measurement corresponding to one thousand billion terabytes. The **terabyte** (To) is itself estimated in thousands of Gigabyte. The yottabyte is used in particular for very **high-capacity** software. In order of increasing size, the list is the following : Terabyte (TB), Petabyte (Po), **Exabyte** (Eo), Zettabyte (Zo) and Yottabyte. Several large companies have already exceeded the Exabytes for their internal storage. Given the strong growth in the sector, we could perhaps **be looking at a Yottabyte** by **2040**.

CLASSIFICATION OF THE DIFFERENT UNITS OF MEASUREMENT IN RELATION TO THE BYTE

There are two (2) models for **encoding the different sizes of** digital **files**: the classic binary system and the international decimal system. On the one hand, the **international system of units**, with its 1 km = 1,000 m, has introduced a series comprising the byte and its multiples, in decimal base. This has given rise to a table of units of **measurement of capacity**, a fragment of which is as follows:

- **1 kilobyte** (kb) = $_{102}$ bytes = 1,000
- **1 megabyte** (MB) = $_{106}$ bytes = 1,000 KB

and so on until :

- **1 zettabyte** (Zo) = 1^{021} bytes = 1,000 Eo
- **1 yottabyte** (Yo) = 1^{024} bytes = 1,000 Zo

On the other hand, the computer system with its binary base and multiples of the byte to the power of 1,024 instead of the power of 1,000 of the decimal base:

- **1 kibyte** (kio) = 2^{10} bytes = 1,024 bytes
- **1 megabyte** (MiB) = 2^{20} bytes = 1 024 kio

and so on until :

- **1 zebabyte** (Zio) = 2^{70} bytes = 1,024 Eio
- **1 yobiabyte** (Yio) = 2^{80} bytes = 1,024 Zio

VI.3.DIRECTORY

In computing, a **directory** is a list of file descriptions. From the point of view of the file system, it is treated like a file whose contents are the list of referenced files. A directory therefore has the same types of properties as a file such as name, size, date, access rights and various other attributes.

ARBORESCENCE

Each file or directory is referenced by another directory, forming a coherent hierarchy, also known as a tree, whose entry point is the root directory. The root is unique on a UNIX-type system, or on a Windows partition (e.g. *C:*).

DESIGNATION AND NAMING

Naming conventions vary from one operating system to another. A specific character is used to separate directories.

WINDOWS

For example, on Windows systems, this character is a *backslash*:
c:\windows\system32\avifile.dll

The *avifile.dll* file is therefore located in the *system32* directory, which in turn is located in the *windows* directory, itself located at the root of the *C:* file system. We say that *windows* is the parent directory of *system32*.
c:\windows\system32 is said to be an "absolute path" because it is a reference which does not take into account the previous position. In contrast, *system32* is a "relative path": this reference assumes that the current directory is *c:\windows*.

VI.4.SUB-DIRECTORY

A subdirectory is a directory located in another directory on a computer file system, used to organise and manage files by grouping them in a hierarchical structure resembling a tree. It allows data to be categorised and organised systematically, making file browsing, retrieval and maintenance more efficient. Subdirectories can contain files as well as additional subdirectories, enabling the creation of a nested organisation that reflects the logical grouping or function of the information contained.

WINDOWS SUBDIRECTORIES

In Windows operating systems, subdirectories are part of the file system hierarchy that organises and stores files and folders. This structure is visually represented in File Explorer, where the C: drive generally serves as the root of the file systems on most personal computers.

Windows uses pathnames to traverse this hierarchy, which can be absolute (specifying the full path from the root directory) or relative

(specifying the path from the current directory). Pathnames in Windows are characterised by backslashes "/" as separators between directory names in a path (unlike the slashes "/" used in Unix-like systems).
Forfor example, the path path "
C:\Users\JohnDoe\Documents\Work\Project1" points to the "Project1" sub-directory in the "Work" directory, which is itself a sub-directory under "Documents" for the user "JohnDoe".

CHAPTER VII

OVERVIEW AND USE OF THE INTERNET

The Internet is a computer network made up of a set of computers interconnected by cables, telephone lines, infrared, etc. and communicating using the same communication language.

Network interconnection is the logical next step in the evolution of technology applied to computing.

All computers, whatever their make or power, can freely exchange information. Over time, the number interconnected computers and their position on the globe evolve, and the topology of the networks resembles the mesh of an immense net, or an immense spider's web.

A machine (computer or connection device) connected to the network is called a network node, or host. A machine that offers services: computing time, documents, database, is a server. The user's machine that uses a service from the host at a given time, i.e. that is being "served", is called a client.

The Internet is currently the largest network in the world. It can be used from any home, thanks to the falling price of home computers, their increasing power and the ease of obtaining software to use it. The Internet is gigantic: no one knows its exact size. It is growing exponentially. The Internet spans every continent. Of course, the density of nodes and servers is not the same in Antarctica as in America.

In any case, it covers rich countries. What's more, the vast majority of services offered on the Internet are (still) free. The idea of "information superhighways" or "information highways" arose from the interactive aspect of the Internet. Users can talk to each other, contribute their experiences and participate freely. Does this mean the Internet for everyone? What are the conditions that would move the idea of information highways from myth to reality? How can we develop the telephone without integrating the computer and its screen, and the same goes for television?

NETWORK DEVELOPMENT

Networks develop from the bottom up. For example: the computers in a laboratory are interconnected, then an inter-network between laboratories creates the local network of the university campus. The departments are connected, then the regions to create a national network, which will then be connected internationally.

This is how the complex mesh of the great interplanetary network is formed.

Communication protocols
The same communication language is needed for all the computers in the world, called the vehicular language. TCP/IP is the common language spoken by all workstations to communicate with each other, and with network equipment (for example, routers that interconnect different physical links and ensure that data is transmitted in the right direction). TCP/IP (Transmission Control Protocol/Internet Protocol)
Refers to a set of communication protocols on which many applications are based.
The basic protocol, IP (Internet Protocol), describes a unique address and specifies the attributes of the data packets transferred.
In simple terms, the basic principles are as follows:
EACH STATION HAS AN ADDRESS
To be clearly identified and able to exchange information, each computer connected to the Internet is allocated a unique IP address. This is true both for a server that has a fixed link to the network, and for a consultation terminal that obtains an address each time it connects, taken at random from the access 's "stock" of addresses (a company that has a fixed link to the network, has an IP address and has obtained the right to be an IP address).
An IP address or IP number is unique in the world. Addresses are allocated by the NIC (Network Information Centre).
The IP address indicates the network number, the subnetwork number (if any) and the host number (the machine). However, this numbering cannot be used to identify the country or continent in which the station is located.
This address is made up of 4 bytes written in decimal form, separated by dots. For example 129.145.16.2
INTRODUCTION TO THE INTERNET
One of the first Internet services, created in 1983, the DNS (Domain Name System) is installed on certain dedicated machines. This service updates a table of correspondence between the IP number of an Internet node and an associated, unique name. It is a sort of distributed directory on the Internet, converting name to IP address.
For example: ftp.univ-rennes.fr is equivalent to 129.20.254.1. The DNS works in a tree structure, based on the principle of zones and sub-zones.
In the name equivalent to the IP address, the name of the zone, the hierarchical superior, gives an indication of where the site belongs, for example: fr for France.

Meshing and dynamic data routing.

A network is a set of nodes and links.

IP networks are made up of stations, physical links (cables, dedicated links, etc.) and active network equipment (routers). A router provides the interconnection between several physical links. It has an addressing table (routing table) which indicates, for each destination IP number, the next router to which it should send messages (data).

Information on changes to all networks is updated in real time by the routers, which communicate with each other using routing protocols. If a particular link is cut or destroyed between two users, the routers adapt and another route is chosen, in real time.

The advantage of this technique is that, if a route is congested or breaks down, the messages take other paths. It doesn't matter if these paths are longer, because at the speed of electrical signals or light, the effective transit time for information is short.

Data is transmitted in packets, called datagrams.

In addition to the data (a few thousand characters), each datagram contains the address of the sending station and the address of the receiving station. Packets also indicate their size, which part of the original document they carry and a means of checking their integrity. Packets circulate in the network, through links and routers, independently of each other, even if they belong to the same original document.

CHAPTER VIII

WEBSITES AND CATEGORIES

VIII.1.INTERNET SITES

DEFINITION

A website is a collection of web pages hosted on a server and linked together by hypertext links. Websites are accessible to Internet users via a web browser. They generally consist of static content (text, images, videos, etc.) and/or dynamic content (forms, databases, etc.). Websites can be created and managed by individuals or companies.

Websites can be divided into 3 main categories: static websites, dynamic websites and application-based websites. Static websites contain only HTML pages and static images. Dynamic websites are generated from databases and are more interactive. Application-based websites are websites that run web applications and special services such as forums, blogs, etc.

Websites can be created using different web technologies such as HTML, CSS, JavaScript, PHP, ASP, etc. These technologies can be combined to create complex, interactive websites. Websites can also be developed using CMS (Content Management Systems), which are easy-to-use content management systems that allow users to update and manage their website without any specific coding knowledge.

Websites can be hosted on remote servers or on local servers. Sites hosted on remote servers are generally more expensive and more difficult to administer, but offer faster loading speeds and greater security. Sites hosted on local servers are cheaper and easier to manage, but offer slower loading speeds and less security.

THE PURPOSE OF A WEBSITE

A website is used to share information with the world. It can be used to promote products and services, provide information about a company or organisation, create communities and offer entertainment. Websites can also be used to sell products and services, collect data, raise funds and much more.

Any company, public body, organisation, association or individual can create a website with varying degrees of technical expertise and knowledge. Today, the Internet is made up of billions of websites created by billions of different people. You can even create a website or blog on the Internet. See the section below on website types for a list of the types of website categories.

VIII.2.CATEGORIES OF WEBSITES

1. SITE VITRINE

Presents the company or brand and its activities. The form is free and this type of site generally has an original layout.

2. CATALOG SITE

Presents the company or brand, its activities and all its products in detail.

3. INFORMATION SITE

Brings together data on a common subject.

4. E-COMMERCE WEBSITE

Dynamic online shop with content management and secure payment integration.

5. INSTITUTIONAL WEBSITE

Describes an organisation, its activities and its values. The corporate site provides all the practical information needed by its customers or beneficiaries. It can also be used to put economic players such as local authorities and associations in touch with each other.

6. THE INTRANET

Accessible only to staff of the same company or department, the intranet makes professional information available and shares it.

7. MINI-SITE - COMPETITIONS - EVENTS

A mini-site is attached to a corporate site or a brand and can be used to create a dynamic and promote a particular event.

CHAPTER IX

WEB BROWSERS AND SEARCH ENGINES

IX.1.INTERNET BROWSERS

Web browsers are software programs **for browsing the Internet and displaying web pages**. To use them, **your hardware must be connected to the Internet**. There are many free browsers, but **some protect your personal data better**. We recommend that you install several browsers on your device, as some sites work better on one or other. Finally, to get the most out of them, you should **update them regularly**.

THE 6 MAIN WEB BROWSERS

Chrome: developed by Google

Developed by **Google** in 2008, it runs on most operating systems: Windows, macOS, Linux, Android and iOS/iPadOS.

Users generally appreciate its speed of use and the many features, applications and extensions available.

Safari: Apple only

Distributed by **Apple** and available only for Apple products (macOS, iOS, iPadOS).

Safari claims to be extremely fast and customisable. Apple provides Safari on all its devices. You don't normally need to download it.

Mozilla Firefox: securing personal data

Developed by the Mozilla Foundation and its many volunteers. It is available on most operating systems. It also has a wide range of **features** and **extensions**, and is renowned for its **protection of personal data**.

Edge: published by Microsoft

Web browser from **Microsoft,** pre-installed on Windows devices. It has been available since 2015 and replaces Internet Explorer, which is no longer updated and therefore not secure. Microsoft Edge also runs on macOS, Android and iOS.

It also has **built-in tools** to help you with your online purchases.

Opera: integrates a VPN

Created in 1995, Opera is a Norwegian browser that runs on Windows, Linux, macOS, iOS and Android. It was one of the first to introduce **tabs** to make browsing easier. Its advantage? It has a **built-in VPN** for secure browsing.

Brave: ad-free and privacy-friendly

Brave is **a free, open source software that** focuses on **protecting privacy** by blocking trackers and ads by default. It runs on Windows, Linux, macOS, iOS and Android.

NB:

- *To install a web browser,* ***download it, then double-click*** *the installation file on your device to launch it. Then* ***follow the instructions****.*
- *The address bar is often confused with the search box. Here you can enter the address of a website or web page to access it directly. You can also type in keywords to launch a search. In this case, a page of results will be displayed, from the search engine selected by default on your browser.*

IX.2.SEARCH ENGINES

A **search engine** is a application that enables users to carry out a **local** or **online search**, i.e. to find resources based on a query made up of terms. Resources can include web pages, Usenet forum articles, images, videos, files, books, educational sites, applications and open source software.

In principle, they generally work as follows:

- with indexing of website content in one or more databases of the search engine operator, indexing being carried out prior to the search.

- Depending on its parameters (e.g. Google's different search algorithms), the search engine returns a list of pages corresponding to the words searched for.

Some websites offer a search engine as their main feature; the site itself is referred to as a "search engine". These are web without human intervention, which distinguishes them from directories. They are based "robots", also known as "*bots*", "*spiders*", "*crawlers*" or "agents", which automatically scan sites at regular intervals to discover new addresses (URLs). They follow the hypertext links that connect pages to each other, one after the other. Each page identified is then indexed in a database,can then be accessed by Internet users using keywords.

Websites offering directories of websites are also referred to as "search engines": in this case, they are search tools developed by people who list and classify websites deemed worthy of interest, not indexing robots.

Search engines don't just apply to the Internet: some engines are software installed on a personal computer. These are so-called "desktop" search engines that combine searching among files stored on the PC and searching among websites - examples include Copernic Desktop Search, Windex Server, etc.

There are also meta-engines, i.e. websites where the same search is launched simultaneously on several search engines, with the results then merged to be presented to the web user.

SOME LEADING SEARCH ENGINES

We could have talked about the "best search engines", but on **the** search **engine market, quality is not synonymous with success.**

What are the 5 most popular search engines?

In 2024, Google, Bing, Yahoo, Baidu and Yandex are the most widely used search engines worldwide.

In 2024, the market will be dominated by tech giants such as Google, Microsoft and Yahoo, and by national search engines where Google is banned, notably in China and Russia. In this first part, you will find the leading search engines in terms of market share.

Disclaimer: the figures vary enormously from one study to another. To give you an example, for Google we found a market share ranging from 86% to 94% worldwide... We have therefore chosen to select the results of the most recent studies (in 2023, the figures for 2024 are not yet available) proposed by **Statista and StatCounter**, even if some inconsistencies persist, as we shall see.

1. Google, the market-leading search engine with 84.69% market share

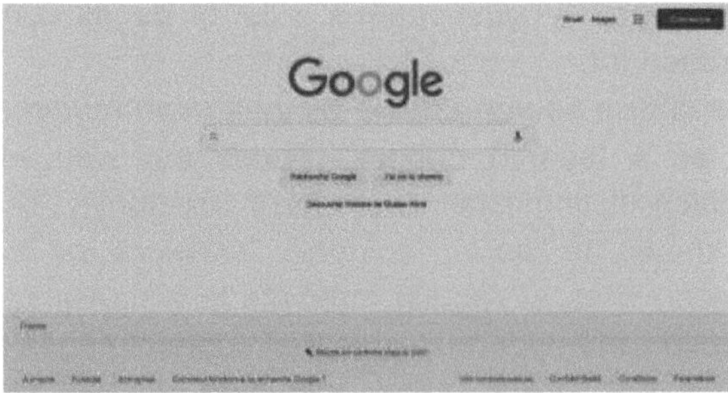

The **American search engine** Google is the undisputed market leader. With more than 80% of the global market share in 2024**, Google has a virtual monopoly**.
Do we still need to introduce the American ogre? Easily recognisable by its sleek design and search bar, the company is regularly criticised for its use of user data, but remains by far the most widely used search engine on the internet.
However, its ease of use and the quality of its algorithm make it a must-have not only for its users, but also for all SEO (Search Engine Optimization) professionals, and it is hard to find a better search engine.
2. Bing, Microsoft's search engine

Bing or Microsoft Bing is the second largest search engine. Microsoft's search engine is Google's number 1 competitor and is keeping its other rivals at bay thanks to a competitive advantage: **Bing is the default search engine on Windows PCs**.
Bing is fairly close to Google in terms of functionality, and we really like the search engine's wallpaper photos, which make it much more user-friendly than its competitors.
Bing is clearly underestimated and remains in the shadow of Google

despite numerous improvements and new features in recent years. Bing, for example, offers more and more tools for SEO and advertising professionals, and is a step ahead of AI thanks to OpenAI and ChatGPT.

3. Yahoo, the old-timer that's putting up a fight

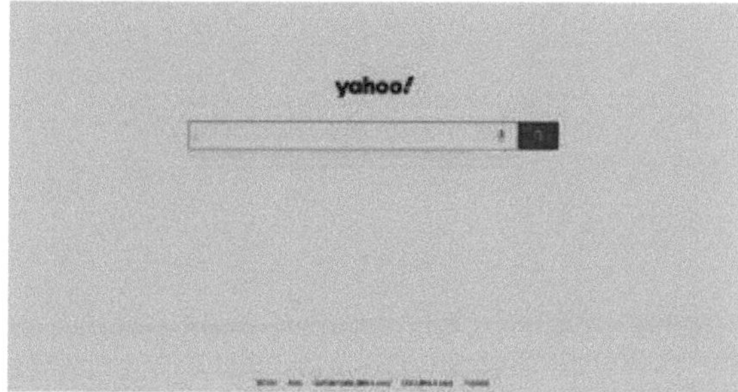

The youngest among us remember the days when Yahoo was better known and used than Google. You have to go back a long way to remember, but Yahoo was created before Google and had its moment of glory before slowly losing market share.

After having tried to buy Google in 2000 and then the social network Facebook in 2006, after having come close to being bought by Microsoft in 2008 for 47 billion dollars, it was Verizon that acquired the search engine **for "only" 4.8 billion dollars**. Despite these ups and downs, Yahoo is still the world's 3rd largest Internet search engine, accounting for 2.59% of global search queries.

4. Baidu, China's number 1 search engine

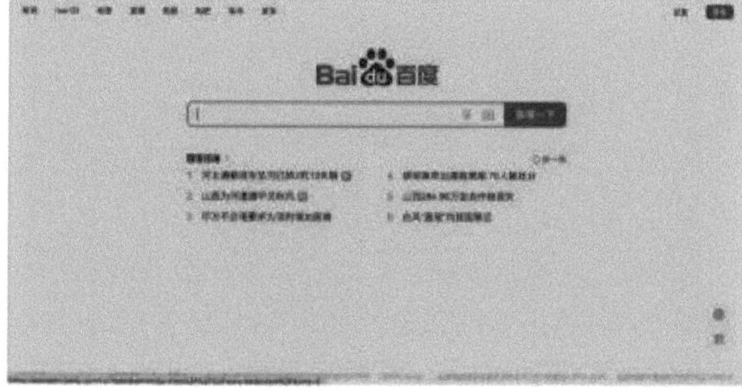

Google's power is worrying some countries that have banned it. This is the case in China, which uses the Baidu , search enginecreated in 2000, to the tune of over 70%.

The advantage using an internet search engine other than Google is it is easier to censor certain information on the web. **But that hasn't stopped the Chinese search engine from establishing itself as the**

world's 4th largest search engine, with a host of additional features for internet searches.

5. Yandex, the Russian search engine

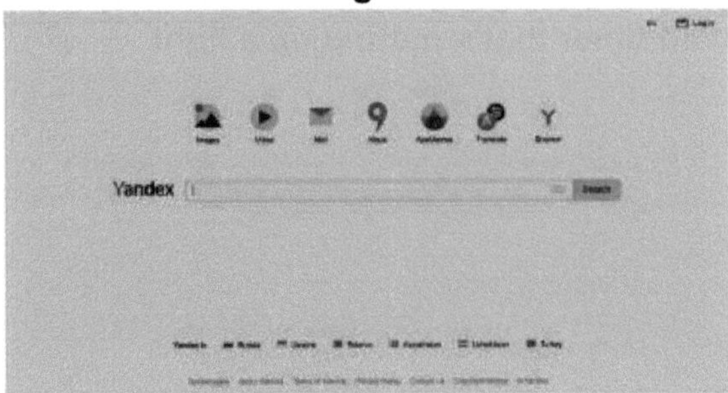

Same causes, same consequences. While Google is not banned in Russia, it is not the market leader, since the Russian search engine Yandex has over 60% of the market share.

Created before Google (in 1997), **Yandex** is similar to Baidu, **offering features similar to those of Google**, such as video search, image search, translation and the possibility having an email address.

A veritable bombshell in the world of search engines (a small world, I agree), Yandex was bought for 5.2 billion dollars in 2024 against a backdrop of war between Russia and Ukraine, explained in this excellent article by Zone Bourse.

CHAPTER X

ELECTRONIC MESSAGING

X.1.DEFINITION

Electronic *mail* refers to the service of transferring messages sent by an electronic messaging system *via* a computer network (now the Internet) to the electronic mailbox of a recipient chosen by the sender. "Correspondence service enabling electronic messages to be exchanged via a computer .network ".

Email, a contraction of the words **courrier** and **électronique**, also refers to the message exchanged by this means according to the official terminology of the French language.

X.2.CREATING AN E-MAIL ADDRESS

First, choose a Google Account type

This account will be for me or to run a business

NB: When you create a Google Account for your business, you can activate personalisation for businesses. A business account also makes it easier to configure the Google business , listingwhich helps to improve the visibility of your business and manage your information online.

When you create a Google Account, you'll be asked for personal information. By providing accurate information, you help to secure your account and make our services more useful to you.

Also if you don't need a Gmail account to create a Google Account. You can use an email address other than Gmail to create one.

1. Go to sign in to your Google Account.
2. Click on **Create an account**.
3. Enter your name.
4. In the "User name" field, enter a user name.
5. Enter your password and confirm.

NB: When you enter your mobile password, the first letter is not case-sensitive.

6. Click **Next**.

o Optional: Add a telephone number to your account, then confirm.

7. Click **Next**.

USE AN EXISTING E-MAIL ADDRESS

1. sign in to your Google Account.
2. Click on **Create an account**.
3. Enter your name.
4. Click on **Use my current e-mail address instead**.
5. Enter your current e-mail address.

6. Click **Next**.

7. Validate your e-mail address using the code sent to your existing e-mail address.

8. Click on **Validate**.

X.3.CREATING A YAHOO ADDRESS

To **create a yahoo.co.uk email address**, go to the **Yahoo** home page from your browser.

1. Go to the Yahoo login page or type the URL login.yahoo.com
2. Click on the "Create an account" button at the bottom right of the page
3. Fill in the required information: first name, surname, telephone number, gender, date of birth, etc. Boxes marked with an asterisk must be filled in. Choose an **e-mail address** and a strong password to protect your personal data.

X.4.CREATING A HOTMAIL ADDRESS

Since Hotmail became Outlook.com, it has become less easy to create an account. If you already have an *@hotmail.fr*, *@hotmail.com* or *@msn.com* internet address, you will automatically be redirected to the login.live.com address, i.e. the one leads to the new Outlook version of the Hotmail mailbox.

Here are a few simple steps to access this amazing mail service.

1. You'll need to visit **outlook.com**.
2. The next thing you need to do is click on the "Create a free account" button at the bottom, which will take you to the registration page.
3. When you receive a new e-mail address, you will then be able to choose your domain name, i.e. *@outlook.fr* or *@hotmail.fr.*

Enter

4. You will need to enter a username and password, which will now be used to **access Hotmail**. Microsoft will then ask you whether or not you

wish to receive promotional e-mails. You will then choose whether or not you wish to receive promotional emails from Microsoft.

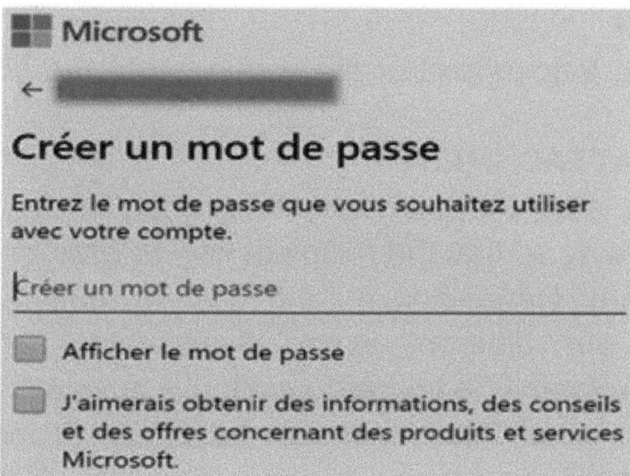

5. Microsoft will then ask you for some important information such as your name, your date of birth, your gender, your telephone number in case you forget your password, your place of residence... Of course, Hotmail guarantees the protection of your data

6. Next, Microsoft will probably ask you to confirm that you are not a robot by entering the characters you see.

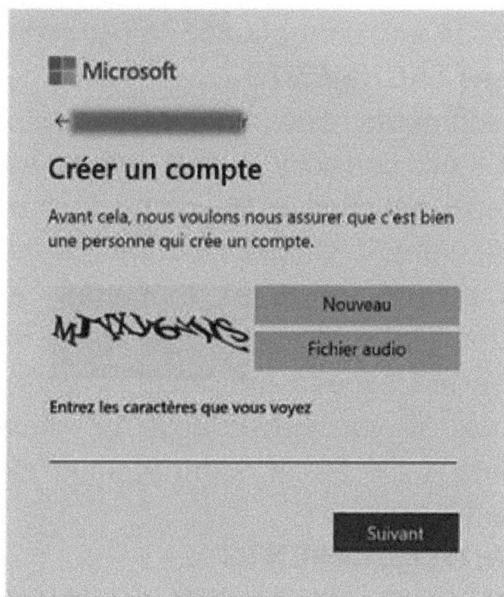

7. Once you've entered your details, you'll need to click on your request and confirm it, which will be the final step in **obtaining the Hotmail account**.

8. Click and confirm. Verification will be sent to you by text or email to ensure that **your Hotmail account is created** and in safe hands.

CHAPTER XI

ATTACHMENTS

XI.1.DEFINITION

An attachment is a document or file appended to the body of an e-mail message.

XI.2.INDICATE ATTACHMENTS

When sending a letter with attachments or enclosures, it is important to indicate them clearly so that the recipient knows what to expect and how to deal with them. Depending on the type of letter and the delivery method, there are different ways of indicating attachments and enclosures. For example, if you are sending a business letter by post or courier, you can write "Attachment(s)" or "Encl." at the bottom of the letter, followed a list of attached documents or files. If you are writing a cover letter sent by post or courier, you can write "Attachment(s)" or "Encl." at the bottom of the letter, followed by the name of the document or file that is attached. Alternatively, if you are sending an e-mail or using an online platform, you can write "Attachment(s)" or "Attachment" at the end of your message, followed by a list of documents or files attached. You can also use the subject to indicate the attachments; for example, "Subject: Invoice" #1234 and contract #5678 (Attached)".

XI.3.FORMATTING ATTACHMENTS

When sending attachments and enclosures with your letter, it is necessary to format them correctly to make them easy to identify, open and read. Use a clear, descriptive file name that matches the content and purpose of the document. Choose a common, compatible file format such as PDF, DOCX, JPG or XLSX that your recipient can access without any problems. In addition, make sure that the file size is reasonable and does not exceed the limits of your delivery method or your recipient's inbox. If you have large or multiple files, consider compressing them into a ZIP file or using a cloud storage service or file sharing platform to send them.

XI.4.FOLLOW-UP WITH RECIPIENTS

After sending your letter with attachments or enclosures, you may want to follow up with your

recipients to confirm that they have received and examined them. This can help you avoid any misunderstandings, delays or missed opportunities. Therefore, it's important to wait a reasonable amount of time before following up - depending on the urgency and importance of your letter and attachments or enclosures, this could take a few days or a week. Also, use the same or a similar delivery method as your original letter. When sending the follow-up message, be sure be polite and respectful; thank your recipient for their time and attention, remind them of the purpose and content of your letter and attachments or enclosures, and ask if they have any questions, comments or actions to take.

XI.5.MANAGING RECIPIENT RESPONSES

When you receive a response from your recipient after following up with them, it's important to handle it professionally. Depending on the type and tone of the response, you may need to acknowledge and appreciate their reply, answer their questions or respond to their comments, or confirm or request next steps or actions. For example, if they have agreed or requested next steps, you should confirm them accordingly. On the other hand, if they have questions or comments about your letter and attachments, provide clear and precise answers or explanations. In addition, thank them for their interest, cooperation or approval. This will help ensure a positive outcome.

CHAPTER XII

OVERVIEW AND BASICS OF MICROSOFT WORD

XII.1. LAUNCHING MS WORD

There are different ways of launching MS Word.

A. WITH THE START MENU

The most conventional way to launch Word is from the Start menu. Click successively on

Start> ***All programmes***> ***Microsoft Office***> ***Microsoft* Word** (see figure below)

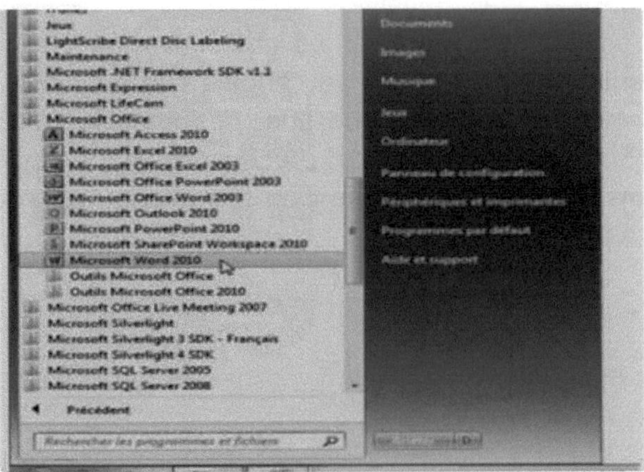

B. STARTING FROM THE DESKTOP

If you have a Word icon on your Windows desktop, you can double-click on it to open the application (see figure below).

XII.2. SUMMARY DESCRIPTION OF THE RIBBON

To use Word properly, it is important to understand its interface, i.e. the various elements that make up the application window (see figure below).

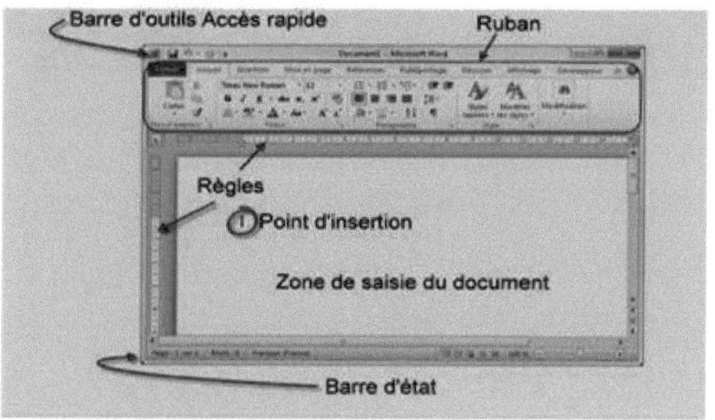

XII.3. CREATING A NEW DOCUMENT

XII.3.1. NEW WORD DOCUMENT

The document entry area occupies the central part of the window. A flashing vertical bar, called the "insertion point", indicates where the next character typed on the keyboard will appear. If the input area is not large enough to display the entire document, you can use the vertical and horizontal scrollbars to move around the document (see figure below).

XII.3.2. DISPLAY OF THE RULE

You can easily display the ruler in Word and hide it. Microsoft Word provides you with a ruler that you can use to define tabs in a document. To display or hide the ruler in Microsoft Word, first select the **"View"** tab in the Ribbon. Then check or uncheck the "**Ruler**" box in the "**Display**group to activate or deactivate the display of the ruler. Tick the box to display the ruler. Unchecking the box hides the ruler.

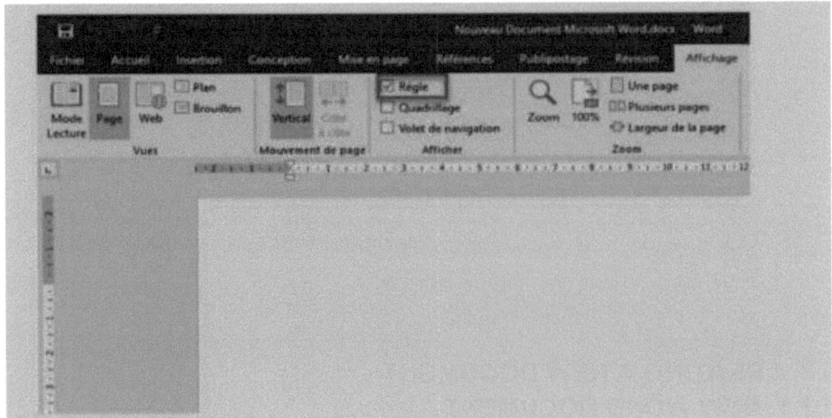

XII.3.3. TEXT INPUT

To enter text, simply type the required text into the appropriate part of the window. Unlike a typewriter, you don't need to validate at the end of the line, because the line break is automatic. Word takes care of this for you. This is known as "typing by the kilometre". You only validate when you want to create a new paragraph.

To create or change a paragraph, simply press the Enter key twice. The first time, you mark the end of the paragraph and the second time you leave a blank line between the two paragraphs. A paragraph can contain from zero to ... many characters (a space counts as one character, the non-printable character representing it is a small dot.

XII.4. OPENING, SAVING AND CLOSING A DOCUMENT

Provides access to the general functions for controlling and adjusting the software (saving a document, opening, printing, setting options, etc.). We use the Office button for some offices and the File menu for others.

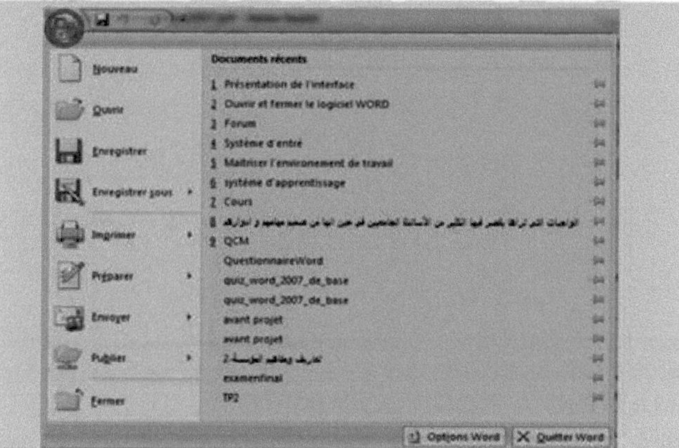

XII.4.1. SAVING CHANGES TO A DOCUMENT

Once you have created a document, don't forget to save it, otherwise you risk losing all your work.

To do this, click on the **Office button** (or **File menu** for some offices) and then on the **Save As** button. You can then choose the save format:

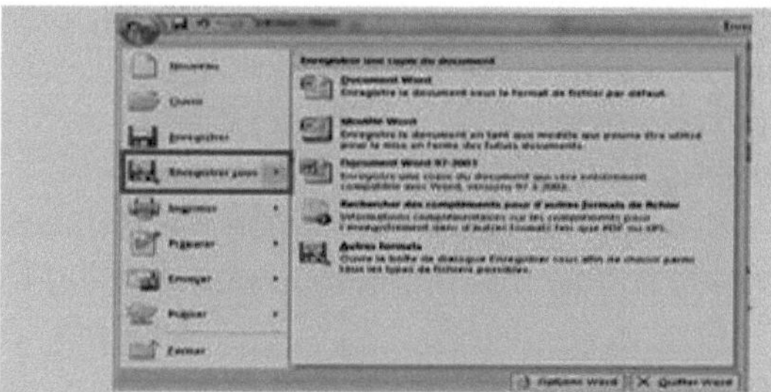

You now need to choose the location where you want to save your file, and specify the file name

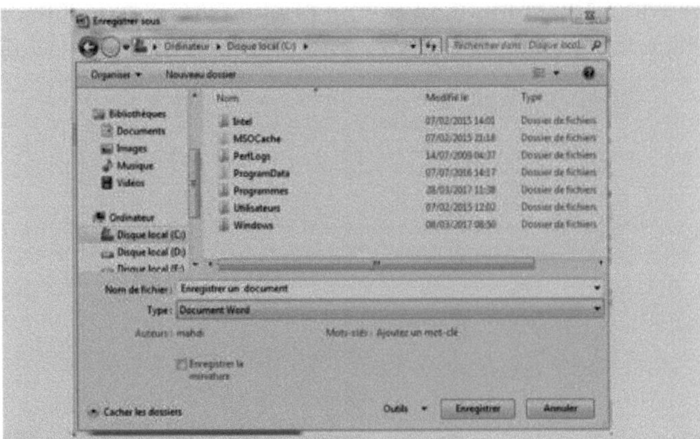

XII.5. FORMATTING A WORD DOCUMENT

XII.5.1. PARAGRAPH FORMATTING

As soon as you press the *Enter key* within a text, you create a new paragraph (empty, if it contains no characters). There are as many paragraphs as there are characters ¶ (displayed when the "Show all" button on the ¶ icon is activated).

To change the *formatting* of *a single paragraph, simply place the cursor in that paragraph.* *in that paragraph*

If not, they need to be selected.

To format paragraphs, you can use :

- *The commands in the Paragraph group*, on the Home tab ;
- *The "Paragraph" window* that appears after activating Paragraph group launcher ;
- *The mini formatting toolbar* ;
- *The horizontal ruler*. If it is not displayed: tick the "Ruler" box in the Show/Hide group on the View tab.

Or, more quickly: click on the tooltip button "Rule", located at the top of the vertical scroll bar.

Withdrawals

There are 4 types of indentation, 3 on the left corresponding to the symbols □ ▽ △ and one on the right △ . :

a) Left indent (i.e. space left on the left, in addition to the margin)

There are three types of left-hand withdrawal:

- *Global indentation* (for all lines): click and drag the indentation □ on the ruler.

The text is aligned with the vertical dotted line.

- *Indent only the 1st line of each paragraph*: click and drag the indent ▽ on the ruler. This formatting is frequently used.
- *Indent all lines except the first line of each paragraph* (opposite to the previous case): click and drag the left indent △ on the ruler.

b) Right indent (i.e. space left on the right, in addition to the margin)

This time, use the right indentation △ on the ruler.

If you find that setting indents with the ruler isn't precise enough, use the 'Paragraph' window: right-click on the selected text > Paragraph > 'Indent and space' tab. Or, more quickly, *double-click on one of the 4 indent symbols on the ruler.*

c) Decrease shrinkage" and "Increase shrinkage" buttons

The "Decrease indent" button and the "Increase indent" button are located in the "Paragraph" group.

Indentation values depend on the position of the tab stops (see section 4 below), which are set at 1.25 cm intervals by default.

d) *Spacing and line spacing*

The *"Paragraph" window* can also be used to define :

- Precise *spacing between* selected *paragraphs*; if you choose a space before and after, they will be added.
- *Line spacing*, with line spacing defining the space *between lines*.

e) *The 4 types of alignment: left, centre, right and justify* are located in the Paragraph group, under the Home tab

Align with indents if they exist, otherwise with the left and right margins.

Use the 4 alignment buttons, **left** , **centre** , **right** and **justify** , located in the Paragraph group, under the Home tab.

The "Justify" mode stretches the text from indent to indent, or from margin to margin.

f) *Line break in the same paragraph*

When you press Enter, a line break occurs (the cursor moves to the next line) and a new paragraph is created.

You can make a line break while remaining in the same paragraph: instead of typing Enter, type Shift + Enter.

The ↵ character is then displayed at the end of the line when the "Display all" ¶ button is activated.

BIBLIOGRAPHY

- **The works**
- Guide in support of the Science Learning Area Curriculum, Year 7th class of basic education, 2018.
- Guillaume PLOUIN, *Cloud computing. Sécurité, gouvernance du SI hybride et panorama du marché,* 4e edition, Dunod, Paris, 2016.
- Jacques LONCHAMP, introduction aux systèmes informatiques, Paris, Dunod, 2017.
- **The websites :**
- https://support.microsoft.com
- https://public.iutenligne.net
- https://www.emaze.com
- https://www.phpeasydata.com

Printed by Books on Demand GmbH, Norderstedt / Germany